T0035056

ENGLISH
FOR EVERYONE
JUNIOR
GRAMMAR GUIDE

Author

Ben Ffrancon Dowds is a freelance writer and literary translator.
He writes textbooks and study guides on a wide range of subjects, including ELT, history, and literature. He also works on general nonfiction books for children and adults. Ben studied Medieval and Modern Languages at the University of Oxford, and has taught English in France and Spain. He has contributed to a number of books in the *English for Everyone* series.

Language consultants

Christelle Wakefield is an educational consultant and editor specializing in ELT for young learners and modern foreign languages. She has taught in Spain, Mexico, and Switzerland, and has worked in educational publishing for over 15 years on course books and materials for students and teachers around the world.

Professor Emerita Susan Barduhn's global career in ELT has been as teacher, trainer, supervisor, manager, author, mentor, assessor, plenary speaker, and international consultant. She has been president of IATEFL; director and co-founder of The Language Center, Nairobi; deputy director of International House, London; Chair of the MATESOL Program at the School for International Training; and is currently a consultant for the British Council, Fulbright, the US State Department, TransformELT, and Consultants-e (TCE).

ENGLISH
FOR EVERYONE
JUNIOR
GRAMMAR GUIDE

Senior Editor Ben Ffrancon Dowds
Senior Art Editor Amy Child
Project Editor Amanda Eisenthal
Illustrators Amy Child, Gus Scott
Managing Editor Carine Tracanelli
Managing Art Editor Anna Hall
Senior Production Editor Andy Hilliard
Senior Production Controller Poppy David
Jacket Design Development Manager Sophia MTT
Senior Jacket Designer Surabhi Wadhwa Gandhi
Jacket Designer Juhi Sheth
Senior Jacket Coordinator Priyanka Sharma-Saddi
DTP Designer Deepak Mittal
Publisher Andrew Macintyre
Associate Publishing Director Liz Wheeler
Art Director Karen Self
Publishing Director Jonathan Metcalf

First American Edition, 2023
Published in the United States by DK Publishing
1745 Broadway, 20th Floor, New York, NY 10019

Copyright © 2023 Dorling Kindersley Limited
DK, a Division of Penguin Random House LLC
23 24 25 26 27 10 9 8 7 6 5 4 3 2 1
001–324353–Nov/2023

All rights reserved.
Without limiting the rights under the copyright reserved above, no part of this publication
may be reproduced, stored in or introduced into a retrieval system, or transmitted, in any
form, or by any means (electronic, mechanical, photocopying, recording, or otherwise),
without the prior written permission of the copyright owner.
Published in Great Britain by Dorling Kindersley Limited

A catalog record for this book
is available from the Library of Congress.
ISBN 978-0-7440-6018-8

DK books are available at special discounts when purchased in bulk for sales
promotions, premiums, fund-raising, or educational use. For details, contact: DK
Publishing Special Markets, 1745 Broadway, 20th Floor, New York, NY 10019
SpecialSales@dk.com

Printed and bound in China

www.dk.com

This book was made with Forest
Stewardship Council™ certified
paper – one small step in DK's
commitment to a sustainable future.
**For more information go to
www.dk.com/our-green-pledge**

Contents

1 Present simple

See also:
Present simple negatives 2
Present simple questions 3

I play the guitar.

⚙ 1.1 How to form: Present simple of regular verbs

Regular verbs follow a common pattern. To make the present simple of regular verbs, use the base form of the verb.
When using them with **he**, **she**, or **it**, add an **s** to the base form.

subject	verb	rest of sentence
I	play	the guitar.

Use the base form of the verb.

TIP!
We use base forms to make lots of different sentences in English. Go to Unit 42 to find out more.

You	play	the trumpet.

Use the base form of the verb.

He She It	plays	the piano.

Add an **s** to the base form of the verb for **he**, **she**, or **it**.

We You They	play	the violin.

Use the base form of the verb.

When to use
Use the **present simple** to talk about facts, opinions, or things that happen regularly.

1.2 Spelling rules: Present simple

For most regular verbs, add an **s** to the end of the base form for **he**, **she**, or **it**.
But for base forms with certain endings, add **es** instead of **s**.

play	watch	finish	go	miss	mix	buzz
↓	↓	↓	↓	↓	↓	↓
plays	**watches**	**finishes**	**goes**	**misses**	**mixes**	**buzzes**

Further examples

He **likes** cake.

She **watches** television in the evening.

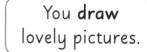

You **draw** lovely pictures.

They **live** in a pink house.

We **read** books every day.

The dog **loves** balls.

1.3 How to form: Present simple of "to be"

To be is an irregular verb in the present simple. It doesn't follow the same pattern as regular verbs.

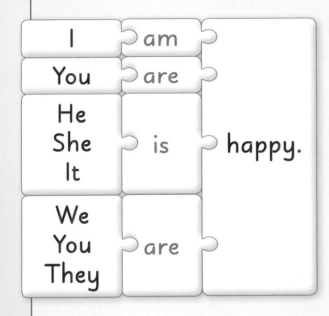

I	am	
You	are	
He She It	is	happy.
We You They	are	

I am happy.

When to use
Use the **present simple** of **to be** to talk about facts, feelings, situations, and states.

Further examples

We **are** friends.

My dad **is** a teacher.

He **is** hot.

They **are** at the park.

You **are** sad.

10

1.4 Present simple: "to be" contractions

We often use contractions of **am**, **is**, and **are**.

I'm ten.

I **am** → I'**m**

You **are** → You'**re**

He **is** → He'**s**

She **is** → She'**s**

It **is** → It'**s**

We **are** → We'**re**

You **are** → You'**re**

They **are** → They'**re**

Further examples

I'**m** cold!

The cat'**s** black.

It'**s** dirty.

We'**re** at school.

They'**re** in the yard.

1.5 How to form: Present simple of "to have"

To **have** is an irregular verb in the present simple. With **he, she,** or **it**, it becomes **has**.

When to use
Use the **present simple** of **to have** to talk about possession, family members, and parts of the body.

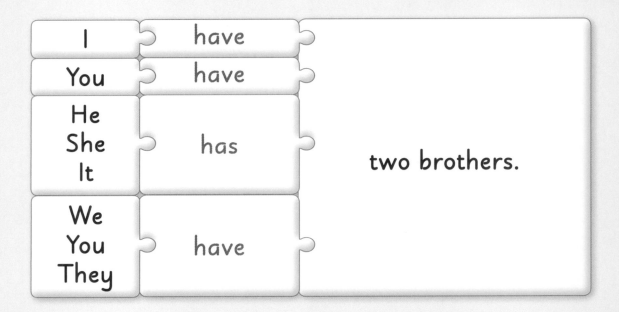

I	have	
You	have	
He She It	has	two brothers.
We You They	have	

I have two brothers.

Further examples

I **have**
a new doll.

She **has**
two books.

We **have**
four balloons.

You **have** some
lemonade.

They **have**
lots of pets.

He **has** a blue
book bag.

It **has** a ball.

We **have** black hair.

Ben **has** a white rabbit.

2 Present simple negatives

See also:
Present simple **1**
Present simple questions **3**

I do not like milk.

2.1 How to form: Present simple negatives

To form the present simple negative of most verbs, put
do not or **does not** before the base form of the main verb.
Never add an **s** to the main verb when forming a negative sentence.

I like milk.

⬇

I do not like milk.

Put **do not** before
the main verb.

She likes milk.

⬇

She does not like milk.

Do not add an **s**
to the main verb.

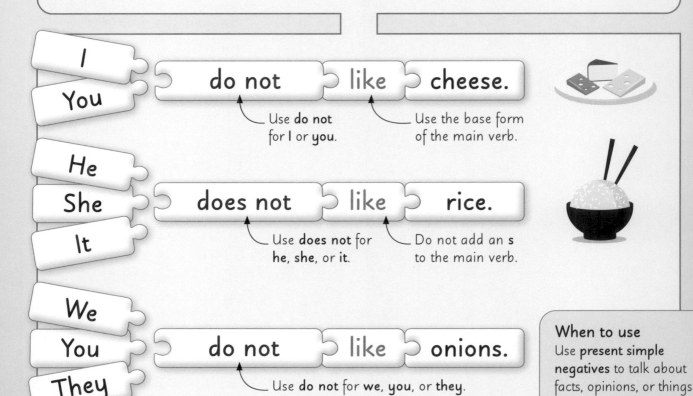

I / You do not like cheese.

Use **do not**
for I or **you**.

Use the base form
of the main verb.

He / She / It does not like rice.

Use **does not** for
he, **she**, or **it**.

Do not add an **s**
to the main verb.

We / You / They do not like onions.

Use **do not** for **we**, **you**, or **they**.

When to use
Use **present simple
negatives** to talk about
facts, opinions, or things
that do not happen.

⚙ 2.2 Present simple negatives: "do not" and "does not" contractions

We often shorten **do not** to **don't** and **does not** to **doesn't**.

do not
↓
don't

does not
↓
doesn't

The two words join together and an apostrophe replaces the o.

Further examples

I **do not enjoy** video games.

It **does not snow** in summer.

He **does not eat** meat.

Sara **doesn't wear** glasses.

They **don't live** in the city.

Tom **doesn't understand** the homework.

⚙ 2.3 How to form: Present simple negatives with "to be"

To form present simple negatives with **to be**, put **not** after
am, **is**, or **are**. You do not need to use **do not** or **does not**.

I am **tired.**

⬇

I am **not** tired.

Put **not** after
am, **is**, or **are**.

I am not tired.

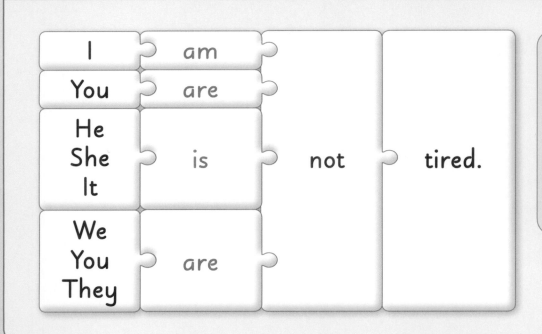

I	am		
You	are		
He She It	is	not	tired.
We You They	are		

When to use
Use **present simple negatives** with **to be** to talk about facts, feelings, situations, or states.

2.4 Present simple negatives: "to be" contractions

There are two ways to shorten the present simple negative of **to be**, except for **I am not**, which only has one contraction.

I am not → I'm not

 You are not → You're not / You aren't

 He is not → He's not / He isn't

 She is not → She's not / She isn't

 It is not → It's not / It isn't

 We are not → We're not / We aren't

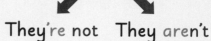 They are not → They're not / They aren't

Further examples

My coat **is not** red.

I **am not** seven.
I am eight.

He **is not** happy.

The robot**'s not** orange, it's blue.

Our house **isn't** big.

The dogs **aren't** dirty.

3 Present simple questions

See also:
Present simple **1**
Forming questions **38**

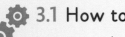 **3.1 How to form: Present simple questions**

For most verbs, add **do** or **does** to the start of a present simple sentence to make it a question. Never add an **s** to the main verb when forming a question.

You play tennis.

⬇

Do you play tennis?

Put **do** at the start of the question.

Put a question mark at the end.

She plays tennis.

⬇

Does she play tennis?

Put **does** at the start of the question.

Do not add an **s** to the main verb.

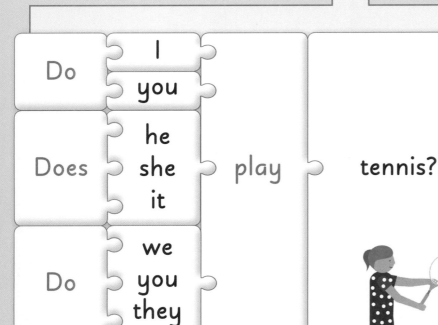

Do	I / you		
Does	he / she / it	play	tennis?
Do	we / you / they		

When to use
Use **present simple questions** to ask about facts, opinions, or things that happen regularly.

Further examples

Do you want some cake?

Do you speak English?

Does she like baseball?

Does he play the guitar every day?

3.2 How to form: Present simple questions with "to be"

To ask present simple questions with **to be**, put **am**, **is**, or **are** before the subject. You do not need to add **do** or **does** to the start.

This is a positive sentence with **to be** in the present simple.

You are **excited.**

Put **are** before the subject, **you.**

Put a question mark at the end.

Are you **excited?**

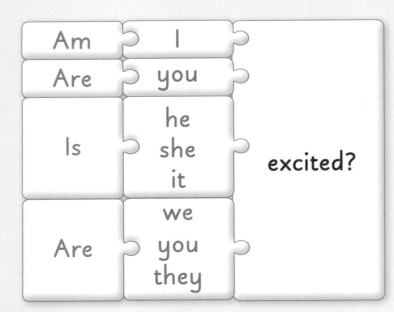

Am	I	
Are	you	
Is	he she it	excited?
Are	we you they	

When to use
Use **present simple questions** with **to be** to ask about facts, feelings, situations, or states.

Are you **excited?**

Yes!

Further examples

Are you awake?

Is he a firefighter?

Is Jenny at home?

Is it cold outside?

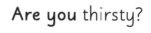

Are you thirsty?

Yes, we are.

Are they at the soccer game?

3.3 How to form: Present simple questions with "to have"

To ask present simple questions with **have** or **has**, add **do** or **does** to the start of the sentence and put **have** in its base form.

This is a positive sentence with **to have** in the present simple.

You have a dog.

⬇

Do you have a dog?

Put a question mark at the end.

Add **do** or **does** to the start of the question

To have is always in its base form.

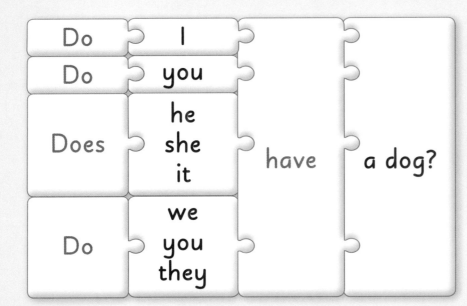

Do	I		
Do	you		
Does	he she it	have	a dog?
Do	we you they		

When to use
Use **present simple questions** with **to have** to ask about possessions, family members, and parts of the body.

Do you have a dog?

Further examples

Does Kate have her hat?

Do you have your coats?

Yes.

Does he have a blue pencil?

Does she have a toothache?

Does Sara have a yellow bike?

Do you have any brothers?

Do we have any homework?

Yes.

4 Present continuous

See also:
Present simple **1**
Infinitives and base forms **42**

I am running.

⚙ 4.1 How to form: Present continuous

To form the present continuous, use **am**, **is**, or **are** after the subject, followed by the present participle of the main verb.

subject	am/is/are	present participle
I	am	running.

Use **am** when you're talking about yourself.

Use the present participle form of the main verb. Present participles always end in **ing**.

You — are — jumping.

Use **are** for **you**.

He
She
It

is — cycling.

Use **is** for **he**, **she**, or **it**.

When to use
Use the **present continuous** to talk about ongoing actions that are taking place in the present moment.

We
You
They

are — walking.

Use **are** for **we**, **you**, or **they**.

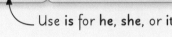

⚙ 4.2 Present participles spelling rules

To form any present participle, add **ing** to a base form. Sometimes, the spelling of the base form changes before we add **ing**.

Final syllable is stressed and last letters are consonant, vowel, consonant.

wear
↓
wearing

For most verbs, just add **ing**.

choose
↓
choosing

Take away the **e**, then add **ing**.

tie
↓
tying

Change **ie** to **y**, then add **ing**.

begin
↓
beginning

Write the last letter twice, unless it's **w**, **x**, or **y**, then add **ing**.

Further examples

I'm painting a picture.

They **are playing.**

REMEMBER!
You can use contractions of the verb **to be**.

I am ➡ I'm

Go to 1.4 to find out more.

Sara **is lying** on the couch.

We're **swimming** in the ocean.

5 Present continuous negatives

See also:
Present simple negatives 2
Present continuous 4

> I am not dancing.

 5.1 How to form: Present continuous negatives

To form present continuous negatives, put **not** after **am**, **is**, or **are**.

I am **dancing.**

↓

I am **not** dancing.

Put **not** after **am**, **is**, or **are**. ⌐ ⌐ The present participle stays the same.

I ⊃ am ⊃ not ⊃ drawing.

Use **am not** for **I**.

You ⊃ are ⊃ not ⊃ eating.

Use **are not** for **you**.

He
She
It ⊃ is ⊃ not ⊃ singing.

Use **is not** for **he**, **she**, or **it**.

We
You
They ⊃ are ⊃ not ⊃ talking.

Use **are not** for **we**, **you**, or **they**.

When to use
Use **present continuous negatives** to talk about something that is not happening in the present moment.

5.2 Present continuous negatives: "to be" contractions

There are two ways to shorten present continuous negatives,
except for **I am not**, which only has one contraction.

I am not → I'm not

You are not → You're not / You aren't

He is not → He's not / He isn't

She is not → She's not / She isn't

It is not → It's not / It isn't

We are not → We're not / We aren't

They are not → They're not / They aren't

Further examples

It **is not raining**!

They **are not studying**.
They are playing.

She **isn't running**.
She's walking.

We're not eating pasta.
We're eating pizza.

6 Present continuous questions

See also:
Present simple **1**
Present continuous **4**

Is it snowing?

Yes!

6.1 How to form: Present continuous questions

To ask present continuous questions, put **am**, **is**, or **are** before the subject.

Put **is** before the subject, **it**.

It **is** snowing.

Is **it** snowing?

Am	I	
Are	you	
Is	he she it	playing?
Are	we you they	

When to use

Use **present continuous questions** to ask whether something is happening in the present moment.

Further examples

7 Present tenses overview

We use both the present simple and the present continuous to talk about the present, but we use them in different situations.

7.1 Present simple

To form the present simple of regular verbs, use the base form of the verb. With **he**, **she**, or **it**, add an **s** or **es** to the base form. Go to Unit 1 to find out more.

Our car is blue.
　　　↳ This is a fact.

> **When to use**
> Use the **present simple** to talk about facts or things that are always true.

I like video games.
　　↳ This is an opinion.

> Use the **present simple** to talk about opinions.

Max reads a book every evening.
　　　↳ This happens regularly.

> Use the **present simple** to talk about habits or things that happen regularly.

7.2 Adding "s" in the present simple

In positive sentences, always add an **s** or **es** to a regular verb for **he**, **she**, or **it**. Never add an **s** or **es** to the verb if it's part of a negative sentence or a question, even if it uses **he**, **she**, or **it**.

He starts school at 9 o'clock.
　　　↳ Add an **s** because the subject is **he** and the sentence is positive.

He doesn't start school at 10 o'clock.
　　　　↳ Do not add an **s** because this is a negative sentence.

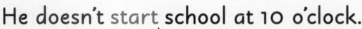

What time does he start school?

　　Do not add an **s** because ↗
　　　this is a question.

7.3 Present continuous

To form the present continuous, use **am**, **is**, or **are** followed by a present participle. Go to Unit 4 to find out more.

I am painting **a picture.**

This is happening in the present moment.

It is snowing.

Use **am**, **is**, or **are** depending on the subject.

They **are riding their bikes.**

Use the present participle form of the main verb.

When to use
Use the **present continuous** to talk about ongoing actions that are taking place in the present moment.

7.4 Comparing the present simple and the present continuous

Use the present simple to talk about habits or things that happen regularly.

Use the **present continuous** to talk about an ongoing action that is happening in the present moment.

We play **table tennis on Mondays.**

We **are playing table tennis.** It's fun!

8 Past simple

See also:
Past simple negatives 9
Past simple questions 10

I washed the car yesterday.

8.1 How to form: Past simple with regular verbs

Regular verbs end with **ed** in the past simple.
The past simple form stays the same for all subjects.

subject	verb	object	time marker
I	washed	the car	yesterday.

Add **ed** to the base form of a verb.

We often use time markers to say when something happened.

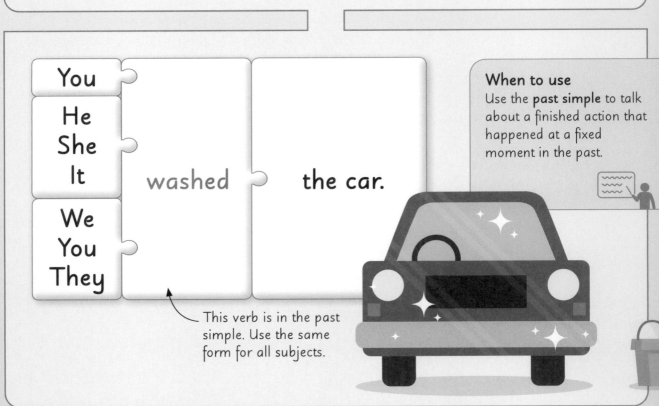

You
He
She
It
We
You
They

washed   the car.

This verb is in the past simple. Use the same form for all subjects.

When to use
Use the **past simple** to talk about a finished action that happened at a fixed moment in the past.

⚙ 8.2 Spelling rules: Past simple

To form the past simple of regular verbs, add **ed** to the base form of a verb. Sometimes, the spelling of the base form changes before we add **ed**.

The last letters are a consonant and y.

The last letters are a vowel and a consonant.

wash
⬇
washed

Add **ed** to most verbs.

dance
⬇
danced

Only add **d**.

try
⬇
tried

Change the y to an i, then add **ed**.

stop
⬇
stopped

Write the last letter twice, then add **ed**.

Further examples

I **cleaned** my bike yesterday.

The bus **stopped** in front of the school.

She **cried** because she **dropped** her toy.

We **danced** at the party last night.

They **planted** a tree last week.

8.3 Common irregular verbs in the past simple

Lots of verbs are irregular in the past simple. They can sometimes look a lot different from their base forms. These are some of the most common irregular verbs in the past simple. For a longer list, go to R19.

go	have	do	put	come	see
⬇	⬇	⬇	⬇	⬇	⬇
went	had	did	put	came	saw

8.4 How to form: Past simple with irregular verbs

As with regular verbs, irregular verbs except **to be** stay the same for all subjects.

| I You He She It We You They | went | to the store yesterday. |

We went to the store yesterday.

8.5 How to form: Past simple with "to be"

In the past simple, **to be** has two forms—**was** and **were**. It is the only verb in the past simple that changes depending on the subject.

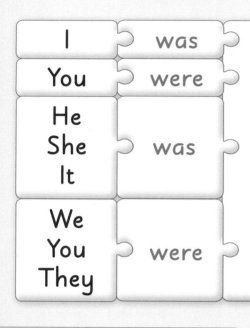

I	was	
You	were	
He She It	was	at the beach last week.
We You They	were	

When to use
Use the **past simple** with **to be** to talk about facts, feelings, situations, or states in the past.

Further examples

Ben **came** to my house last week.

We **had** pasta for dinner last night.

They **were** very tired after school.

9 Past simple negatives

See also:
Past simple 8
Infinitives and base forms 42

I did not like the cake.

⚙ 9.1 How to form: Past simple negatives

To form the past simple negative, add **did not** before the main verb. **Did not** stays the same for all subjects. The main verb always stays in its base form—never use the past simple form or add an **s**.

I liked the cake.

⬇

I did not like the cake.

Add **did not** before the main verb.

The main verb is in its base form.

| I You He She It We You They | did not | like | the cake. |

When to use
Use **past simple negatives** to talk about actions or states that did not happen in the past.

36

9.2 Past simple negatives: "did not" contraction

We often shorten
did not to **didn't**.

I did not like the cake.

⬇

I didn't like the cake.

Did and **not** go together and
an apostrophe replaces the **o**.

Further examples

He **didn't wear** a hat
at the party.

We **did not play** in
the park yesterday.

They **did not
understand** the test.

I **didn't brush** my
hair this morning.

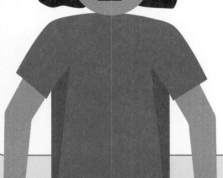

Andy **didn't drink**
his juice.

⚙ 9.3 How to form: past simple negatives with "to be"

To form the past simple negative of **to be**, add **not** after **was** or **were**.
You do not need to use **did not** or **didn't**.

It was **warm.**

⬇

It was **not warm.**

└ Put **not** after **was** or **were**.

It was not warm yesterday.

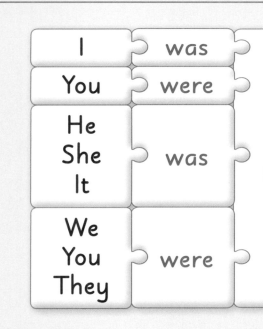

I	was		
You	were		
He She It	was	not	warm.
We You They	were		

When to use
Use **past simple negatives** with **to be** to talk about facts, situations, or states in the past.

Further examples

The dog **was not** hungry.

The store **was not** open.

The balls **were not** red.

⚙ 9.4 Past simple negatives: "was not" and "were not" contractions

We often shorten **was not** to **wasn't** and **were not** to **weren't**.

was **not**

↓

wasn't

Was and **not** go together and an apostrophe replaces the **o**.

were **not**

↓

weren't

Were and **not** go together and an apostrophe replaces the **o**.

Further examples

I **wasn't** very well last week.

The movie **wasn't** interesting.

The questions **weren't** too difficult.

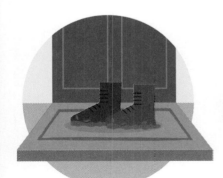

The boots **weren't** clean.

It **wasn't** cold this morning.

The cat **wasn't** white. It was black.

10 Past simple questions

See also:
Past simple 8
Forming questions 38

Did you watch the game?

10.1 How to form: Past simple questions

To ask past simple questions, put **did** before the subject and put the main verb in its base form—do not use the past simple form or add an **s**. **Did** stays the same for all subjects.

You watched **the game.**

⬇

Did you watch **the game?**

Put **did** at the start of the question.

The main verb is in its base form.

Put a question mark at the end.

| Did | I you he she it we you they | watch the game? |

When to use
Use **past simple questions** to ask about completed actions in the past.

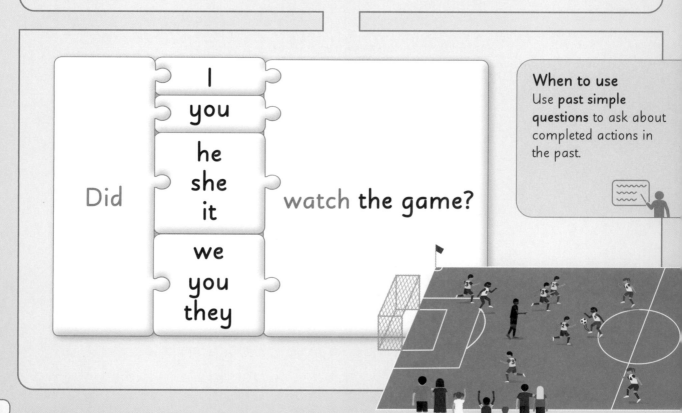

Further examples

Did they catch a fish?

Did she finish the race?

Did you wear a red dress to the party?

Did Jess play soccer today?

Did it rain yesterday?

Did he see a horse at the farm?

Did you go camping last summer?

Did you buy a new hat?

41

10.2 How to form: Past simple questions with "to be"

To ask past simple questions with **to be**, put **was** or **were** before the subject. You do not need to use **did**.

You were at the party yesterday.

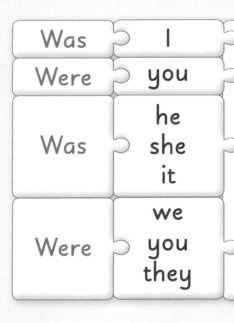

Were you at the party yesterday?

Put **were** before the subject, **you**.

Put a question mark at the end.

Was	I	
Were	you	
Was	he she it	at the party yesterday?
Were	we you they	

When to use
Use **past simple questions** with **to be** to ask about facts, situations, and states in the past.

Were you at the party yesterday?

Yes.

Further examples

Was I fast?

Were you at the park yesterday?

Was the slide big?

Was the clown funny?

Was she excited to see you?

Was school fun today?

Were you scared on the rollercoaster?

Were Dad and Sofia happy to visit Grandma?

11 Past continuous

See also:
Present continuous **4**
Past simple **8**

11.1 How to form: Past continuous

To form the past continuous, use **was** or **were** followed by a present participle.

subject	was/were	present participle	rest of sentence
The sun	**was**	**shining**	**in the sky.**

Use **was** or **were** depending on the subject.

Use the present participle form of the main verb.

11.2 Using the past continuous

There are two ways to use the past continuous.

When to use
Use the **past continuous** to tell a story.

past continuous

The birds were singing in the trees. It was a beautiful day.

Use the **past continuous** to talk about an ongoing action in the past that was interrupted by another action.

past continuous

I was sleeping when an apple fell on my head.

The interrupting action is in the past simple.

Further examples

The boys **were running** through the forest.

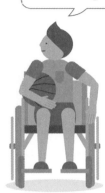

I **was playing** basketball when you called yesterday.

The girls **were having** fun together.

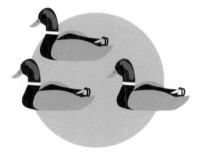

The ducks **were swimming** in the water.

Maria **was listening** to music when Andy arrived.

REMEMBER!
To make most present participles, add **ing** to a base form. Some present participles have different spelling rules. Go to 4.2 to find out more.

It was a cold day. Snow **was falling**.

I **was playing** in the yard when it started to rain.

12 Past continuous negatives

See also:
Past simple 4
Past continuous 11

12.1 How to form: Past continuous negatives

To form past continuous negatives, put **not** after **was** or **were**.

The children were drawing.

⬇

The children were not drawing.

Add **not** after **was** or **were**. ↗ ↖ The present participle stays the same.

12.2 Using past continuous negatives

There are two ways to use past continuous negatives.

When to use
Use **past continuous negatives** to tell a story.

Sara was not listening to music. She was reading a book.

Use **past continuous negatives** to talk about an action that was not happening in the past while another action took place.

I was not paying attention when I fell over the blocks.

↖ The interrupting action is in the past simple.

12.3 Past continuous negatives: "was not" and "were not" contractions

We often shorten **was not** to **wasn't** and **were not** to **weren't**.

 was not **were not**

↓ ↓

wasn't **weren't**

Was and **not** go together and an apostrophe replaces the **o**.

Were and **not** go together and an apostrophe replaces the **o**.

Further examples

The computer **wasn't working**.

It **wasn't raining** when we arrived at the park.

We **were not walking**. We were riding our bikes.

REMEMBER!
To make most present participles, add **ing** to a base form. Some present participles have different spelling rules. Go to 4.2 to find out more.

They **weren't surfing**. They were sailing!

Sofia's mom took a picture, but Sofia **wasn't smiling**.

13 Past continuous questions

Were you playing in your room?

Yes.

⚙ 13.1 How to form: Past continuous questions

To form past continuous questions,
put **was** or **were** before the subject.

Put **were** before the subject, **you.**

You were playing in your room.

Were you playing in your room?

The present participle stays in the same position.

Put a question mark at the end.

Was	I	
Were	you	
Was	he she it	reading?
Were	we you they	

When to use
Use **past continuous questions** to ask about ongoing actions that were happening in the past.

Further examples

Were you jumping rope this morning?

What **was Ben studying** in the library at lunchtime?

Was it snowing at the park?

Was he playing tennis when you saw him?

What **was Dad cooking** when you got home?

What **were you buying** at the store yesterday?

Why **were they whispering**?

Where **was Sara going** yesterday morning?

REMEMBER!
To make most present participles, add **ing** to a base form. Some present participles have different spelling rules. Go to 4.2 to find out more.

14 Present perfect

See also:
Prepositions of time **74**
Irregular verbs **R19**

I have finished **dinner.**

14.1 How to form: Present perfect

To form the present perfect, use **have** or **has** followed by a past participle.

subject	have/has	past participle	rest of sentence
I	have	finished	dinner.

Use **have** or **has** to make the present perfect.

To make past participles of regular verbs, add **ed** to a base form.

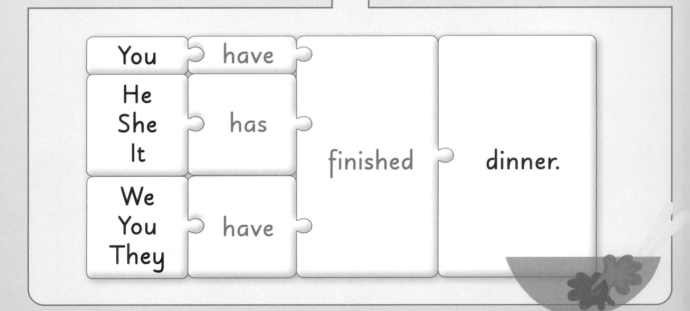

You	have		
He She It	has	finished	dinner.
We You They	have		

14.2 Using the present perfect

There are five ways to use the present perfect.

 I have finished lunch.

When to use
Use this tense to give news or talk about recent events without specifying when they happened.

 I have visited the museum five times.

Use this tense to talk about repeated actions in the past.

 Oh no! I have dropped my keys!

Use this tense to talk about actions or states in the past that have a connection to the present moment.

 I have painted three pictures this morning.

Use this tense to talk about an action that has happened during a period of time that has not finished yet.

 I have studied English for two years.

⌐ We often use **for** and **since** with the present perfect.

Use this tense to talk about an action or state that started in the past, continued into the present, and may continue into the future.

14.3 Present perfect: "To have" contractions

We often use contractions of **have** and **has**.

I have	You have	He has	She has	It has	We have	You have	They have
⬇	⬇	⬇	⬇	⬇	⬇	⬇	⬇
I've	You've	He's	She's	It's	We've	You've	They've

⚙ 14.4 Spelling rules: Past participles of regular verbs

To make the past participle of regular verbs, add **ed** to a base form.
Sometimes, the spelling of the base form changes a little before we add **ed**.

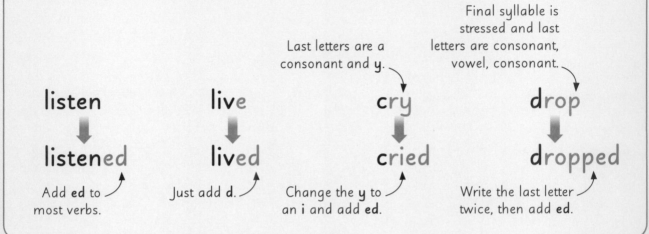

Last letters are a consonant and y.

Final syllable is stressed and last letters are consonant, vowel, consonant.

listen
⬇
listened

Add **ed** to most verbs.

live
⬇
lived

Just add **d**.

cry
⬇
cried

Change the y to an i and add **ed**.

drop
⬇
dropped

Write the last letter twice, then add **ed**.

Further examples

She's **lived** in this house since 1975.

We've **arrived** in New York.

I've **watched** two movies this evening.

Claire **has joined** the soccer team.

I **have invited** my friends to my party.

14.5 Past participles of irregular verbs

Lots of verbs in English have irregular past participles that don't end in **ed**. These are some of the most common irregular past participles. For a longer list, go to R19.

go	be	have	do	come	see
⬇	⬇	⬇	⬇	⬇	⬇
gone	been	had	done	come	seen

 ### 14.6 "Gone" and "been"

Gone is the past participle of **to go**. **Been** is the past participle of **to be**.
We use both to talk about going somewhere, but they mean different things.

Sara has gone to Spain.

This means that Sara is still in Spain.

Sara has been to Spain.

This means that Sara went to Spain, but she isn't there now. She has returned.

Further examples

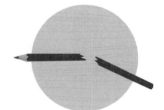

Look! You**'ve broken** your pencil!

Oh no! Andy **has forgotten** his book.

Maria is sad. She **has lost** her doll.

15 Present perfect negatives

See also:
Adverbs of time 69
Prepositions of time 74

⚙ 15.1 How to form: Present perfect negatives

To form present perfect negatives, put **not** between **have** or **has** and the past participle.

I have **been to the beach this year.**

⬇

I have **not been to the beach this year.**

Put **not** after **have** or **has**.

Been is the past participle of **to be**.

When to use
To learn when to use the **present perfect**, go to Unit 14.

⚙ 15.2 Present perfect negatives: "Have not" and "has not" contractions

We often shorten **have not** to **haven't** and **has not** to **hasn't**.

have **not** ⬇ haven't

has **not** ⬇ hasn't

Have and **not** go together and an apostrophe replaces the **o**.

Has and **not** go together and an apostrophe replaces the **o**.

Further examples

I **have not eaten** my breakfast yet.

We **haven't watched** television today.

She **hasn't flown** on a plane before.

16 Present perfect questions

See also:
Adverbs of time **69**
Prepositions of time **74**

 16.1 How to form: Present perfect questions

To ask questions with the present perfect,
put **have** or **has** before the subject.

You **have** been on a rollercoaster.

Have you been on a rollercoaster?

└ Put **have** before
the subject, **you**.

When to use
To learn when to use the
present perfect, go to
Unit 14.

Further examples

Have you read
this book?

Has it snowed
today?

Have they finished
their pictures yet?

Have you seen
my teddy bear?

Have you studied
English this week?

17 Past tenses overview

We use the past simple, the present perfect, and the past continuous to talk about the past, but we use them in different situations.

17.1 Past simple

To form most regular verbs in the past simple, add **ed** to a base form. Go to Unit 8 to find out more.

This is a finished action in the past.

We baked ten cookies yesterday.

When to use

Use the **past simple** to talk about a finished action that happened in the past during a period of time that has now finished.

17.2 Present perfect

To form the present perfect, use **have** or **has** followed by a past participle. Go to Unit 14 to find out more.

This action happened during a time period that hasn't finished yet.

We have eaten three cookies today.

When to use

Use the **present perfect** to talk about an action that has happened in the past during a period of time that has not finished yet.

17.3 Comparing the past simple and the present perfect

We baked ten cookies yesterday.

We have eaten three cookies today.

YESTERDAY   TODAY

This happened during a period of time that has now finished.

This has happened during a period of time that has not finished yet. They might eat more cookies today.

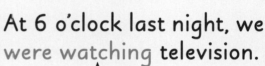

17.4 Past continuous

To form the past continuous, use **was** or **were** followed by a present participle. Go to Unit 11 to find out more.

It was a windy day and leaves were falling from the trees.

This is telling a story about the past.

At 6 o'clock last night, we were watching television.

This is an ongoing action in the past.

When to use
Use the **past continuous** to tell a story.

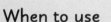

When to use
Use the **past continuous** to talk about an ongoing action in the past.

17.5 Using the past simple and the past continuous together

We were having dinner when the phone rang.

PAST

NOW

The past simple action interrupted the past continuous action.

18 "Going to"

See also:
Present simple **1**
Future tenses overview **25**

18.1 How to form: "Going to"

To form sentences with **going to**, use **am**, **is**, or **are** followed by **going to**, and then the main verb in its base form.

subject	am/is/are	going to	base form	rest of sentence
Sofia	is	going to	win	the race!

Use **am**, **is**, or **are** depending on the subject.

Going to always stays the same.

Don't add an **s** to the base form for **he**, **she**, or **it**.

18.2 Using "going to"

There are two ways to use **going to**.

When to use
Use **going to** to make predictions about the future based on evidence you can see or when you know something is going to happen.

She is going to catch the ball.

Use **going to** to talk about plans or a decision you've already made before the present moment.

I am going to ride my bike to school tomorrow.

Further examples

He **is going to score**.

I'm **going to read** my book later.

They **are going to grow** some flowers.

Oh no! Max **is going to fall over**.

We're **going to play** video games after school.

We **are going to paint** some pictures.

REMEMBER!
You can use contractions
of the verb **to be**.

I am ➡ I'm

Go to 1.4 to
find out more.

Careful! You're **going to drop** the drinks!

Look at the clouds!
It's **going to rain** soon.

19 "Going to" negatives

See also:
Present simple negatives 2
"Going to" 18

19.1 How to form: "Going to" negatives

To make negative sentences with **going to**, add **not** before **going to**.

We are going to arrive on time.

We are not going to arrive on time.

Add **not** before **going to**.

When to use
To learn when to use sentences with **going to**, go to Unit 18.

Further examples

It **is not going to snow** tomorrow.

He **isn't going to play** video games today.

REMEMBER!
There are two ways to shorten **is not** and **are not**. Go to 2.4 to find out more.

They're **not going to find** me!

20 "Going to" questions

See also:
Present simple questions **3**
"Going to" **18**

20.1 How to form: "Going to" questions

To ask questions using **going to**, put **am**, **is**, or **are** before the subject. **Going to** and the main verb stay in the same position.

They **are** going to be late.

Are they going to be late?

Put **are** before the subject, **they**.

When to use
To learn when to use sentences with **going to**, go to Unit 18.

Further examples

Are you going to drink your juice?

Are we going to go to the beach today?

It's very cloudy outside. **Is it going to rain** soon?

Are you going to come to the park later?

Is she going to sing a song?

21 "Will"

See also:
"Going to" 18
Future tenses overview 25

21.1 How to form: "Will"

To form sentences with **will**, use **will** followed by the main verb in its base form. **Will** stays the same for all subjects.

subject	will	base form	rest of sentence
I	will	see	you tomorrow.

Will stays the same for all subjects.

The main verb is in its base form.

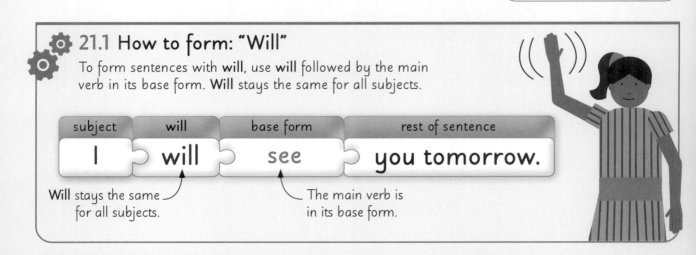

21.2 Using "will"

There are four ways to use **will**.

When to use
Use **will** to talk about a decision you've just made.

I will have a glass of milk.

Use **will** to make a promise.

I will call you when I get home.

Use **will** to make predictions that don't have any evidence in the present moment.

I think you will love this book.

We often use **to think** when making a prediction without evidence.

Use **will** to offer to do something.

I will help you with those bags.

⚙ 21.3 "Will": Contractions

We often shorten **will** to **'ll**.

I will	You will	He will	She will	It will
↓	↓	↓	↓	↓
I'll	You'll	He'll	She'll	It'll

We will	You will	They will
↓	↓	↓
We'll	You'll	They'll

Further examples

I think you**'ll like** this cake. It's chocolate!

That box looks heavy. I**'ll carry** it for you.

I don't like the blue hat, so I**'ll buy** the red one.

I**'ll have** a burger.

We**'ll be** home by 6 o'clock.

22 "Will" negatives

See also:
"Will" 21
"Will" questions 23

 22.1 How to form: "Will" negatives

To form **will** negatives, put **not** after **will**.

Amir will eat his dinner.

Amir will not eat his dinner.

Put **not** after **will**.

When to use
As well as the uses in Unit 21, use **will negatives** when someone or something refuses to do something.

 22.2 "Will" negatives: "will not" contraction

We often shorten **will not** to **won't**.
Won't stays the same for all subjects.

will not

won't

Won't is short for **will not**.

Further examples

You **won't like** this comic book. It's boring!

I **won't be** late, I promise.

The dogs **will not come** inside.

I **won't take** an umbrella with me.

23 "Will" questions

See also:
"Will" **21**
Forming questions **38**

23.1 How to form: "Will" questions

To form questions with **will**, put **will** before the subject.

You **will be** at the concert tomorrow.

Will you be at the concert tomorrow?

Put **will** before the subject, **you**.

When to use
Use **will questions** to ask about the future or to ask someone to do something.

Further examples

Will you call me tomorrow?

Will it be a nice day tomorrow?

Will our team win the game?

Will you take a picture of us, please?

Will you come to my birthday party?

24 Present for future events

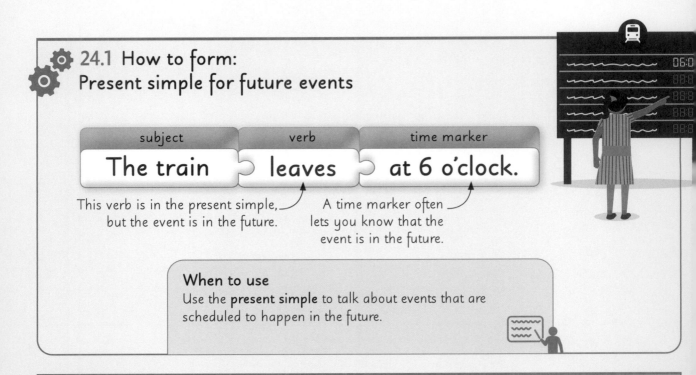

24.1 How to form:
Present simple for future events

subject	verb	time marker
The train	leaves	at 6 o'clock.

This verb is in the present simple, but the event is in the future.

A time marker often lets you know that the event is in the future.

When to use
Use the **present simple** to talk about events that are scheduled to happen in the future.

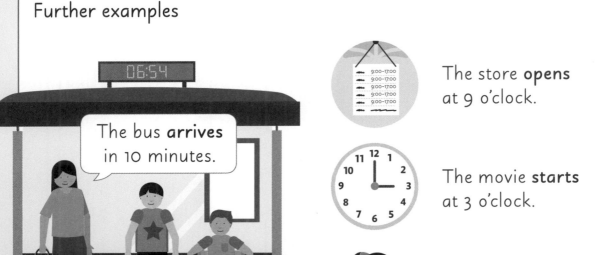

Further examples

The bus **arrives** in 10 minutes.

The store **opens** at 9 o'clock.

The movie **starts** at 3 o'clock.

I **have** band practice this afternoon.

See also:
"Going to" 18
"Will" 21

⚙ 24.2 How to form:
Present continuous for future events

subject	am/is/are	present participle	rest of sentence
I	am	having	pasta for dinner later.

Use **am**, **is**, or **are** depending on the subject.

Use the main verb's present participle form.

 A time marker often lets you know that the event is in the future.

When to use
Use the **present continuous** to talk about future events that are already planned.

Further examples

 I'm **going** to the fair tomorrow.

 They're **playing** badminton after school.

 We're **flying** to Mexico next week.

REMEMBER!
To find out more about forming the present simple, go to Unit 1. To find out more about forming the present continuous, go to Unit 4.

Future tenses overview

We use both **going to** and **will** to make predictions about the future and to talk about decisions we've made, but we use them in different situations. We also use the present tenses to talk about future events.

25.1 Using "going to" and "will" to make predictions

Use **will** to make predictions about the future when there isn't any evidence in the present moment.

Use **going to** to make predictions about the future based on evidence in the present moment.

I think Sara will win the race.

The race hasn't started yet, so there is no evidence that Sara will win.

Look, Sara is going to win the race!

Sara is in front, so there is evidence that she is going to win the race.

REMEMBER!
We also use **will** to make promises and to offer to do something for someone. Go to Unit 21 to find out more.

25.2 Using "going to" and "will" for decisions

Use **going to** to talk about a decision that you have already made before the present moment.

Use **will** to talk about a decision you have just made.

This decision has been made in advance.

This decision was made quickly at the time of speaking.

I'm going to buy a present for Ben.

I know! I will buy him a robot.

25.3 Using the present for future events

To find out how to form the **present simple**, go to Unit 1. To form the **present continuous**, use **am, is,** or **are** followed by a present participle. Go to Unit 4 to find out more.

The museum closes at 8 o'clock today.

When to use
Use the **present simple** to talk about events that are scheduled to happen in the future.

We're having a party tonight.

Use the **present continuous** to talk about future events that are already planned.

26 Imperatives

26.1 How to form: Imperatives

To form imperatives, use the base form of the verb. There is no difference between singular and plural forms. There are no polite or familiar forms.

When to use
Use **imperatives** to tell someone to do something.

base form
Listen!
We often put an exclamation mark after an imperative.

To make imperatives, use the base form of the verb.

base form
Open

rest of sentence
your books, please.

An object can come after the imperative.

Add **please** to make imperatives more polite.

Open your books, please.

See also:
Infinitives and base forms **42**

26.2 How to form: Negative imperatives

To form negative imperatives, add **do not** or **don't** before the base form of the imperative verb.

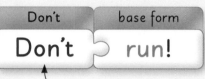

Don't	base form
Don't	run!

To tell someone not to do something, add **don't** before the base form.

Don't	base form + please
Don't	run, please.

When to use
Use **negative imperatives** to tell someone not to do something or to stop doing something.

Further examples

  Sit **down**, please.

  Stand up.

  Stop!

  Help!

 Be careful!

  Don't touch that! It's hot.

  Don't talk, please.

 **Don't worry**, it's okay.

27 "Let's"

Let's take a picture!

⚙ 27.1 How to form: "Let's"

Use **let's** followed by a base form.

Let's	base form	rest of sentence
Let's	take	a picture!

Let's is always in this contracted form.

Sentences with **let's** sometimes end with an exclamation mark.

Let's bake **some cookies.**

Let's learn English!

When to use
Use **let's** to make a suggestion for an activity that includes the speaker.

Further examples

Let's read a book!

Let's go swimming.

Let's play
video games.

Let's buy some
ice cream.

Let's play
in the yard.

Let's go to
the park!

Let's paint the robot's head.

Let's sing and **dance**!

See also:
Short answers **39**
Tag questions **41**

28.1 How to form: Modal verbs

Modal verbs behave differently from normal verbs. They don't change their form depending on the subject. They are usually followed by a main verb in its base form.

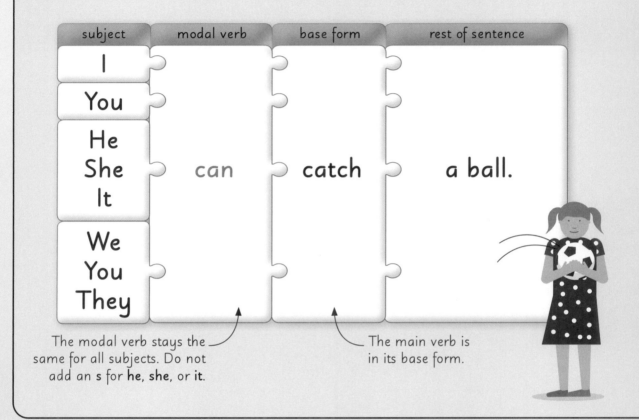

subject	modal verb	base form	rest of sentence
I			
You			
He She It	can	catch	a ball.
We You They			

The modal verb stays the same for all subjects. Do not add an **s** for **he, she,** or **it**.

The main verb is in its base form.

28.2 How to form: Negatives with modal verbs

To make a modal verb negative, put **not** after it.

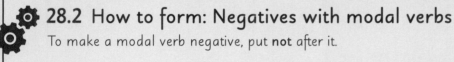

You should wear a coat.

You should **not** wear a coat.

Put **not** after the modal verb.

Using modal verbs

Modal verbs are special verbs in English. We use them to talk about a range of things such as possibility and obligation.

Ability	can	I **can** dance really well.
	could	Maria **could** write her name when she was four.
Requests	may	**May** I have an orange, please?
Permission	may	**May** we sit here?
Advice	should	It's very sunny. You **should** wear a hat.
Suggestions	could	You **could** draw a picture of a flower.
Possibility	might	We **might** go to the zoo today.
	may	I **may** be late to the party.
	could	Don't go outside. You **could** get wet.
Obligations	must	I **must** remember to do my homework.

⚙ 28.3 How to form: Questions with modal verbs

To make questions with modal verbs, put the modal verb before the subject.

You can play baseball.

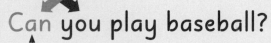

Can you play baseball?

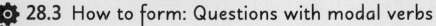
Put the modal verb before the subject.

29 "Can" for ability

⚙ 29.1 How to form: "Can" for present ability

Can is a modal verb. Use **can** followed by the main verb in its base form. Can stays the same for all subjects. Do not add an **s** for **he**, **she**, or **it**.

subject	can	base form	rest of sentence
I	can	play	the piano.

Use the base form of the main verb.

When to use
Use **can** to talk about things someone or something is able to do.

⚙ 29.2 How to form: Negatives with "can"

To form the negative of **can**, add **not** to the end of **can** to form **cannot**. We often shorten **cannot** to **can't**. **Cannot** and **can't** stay the same for all subjects.

I can play the piano.
↓
I cannot play the piano.

Cannot is one word. We often shorten it to **can't**.

When to use
Use **cannot** or **can't** to talk about things someone or something is not able to do.

⚙ 29.3 How to form: Questions with "can"

To ask questions with **can**, put **can** before the subject.

You can play the piano.

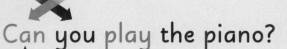

Can you play the piano?

Put **can** before the subject, **you**.

When to use
Use questions with **can** to ask if someone or something is able to do something.

See also:
"Might," "may," and "could" 32
"Could" for suggestions 33

Further examples

I can paint pretty flowers.

They **can read**.

It **can catch** a ball.

The tortoise **cannot walk** fast.

He **can't sing** very well.

She **can't hear** the music.

Can you **see** me?

Can he **ski**?

Can she ride a bike?

29.4 How to form: "Could" for past ability

Could is the past form of **can**. Use **could** followed by the main verb in its base form. **Could** stays the same for all subjects. Do not add an **s** for **he**, **she**, or **it**.

subject	could	base form	rest of sentence
We	could	see	the moon last night.

└─ **Could** stays the same for all subjects.

When to use
Use **could** to talk about things someone or something was able to do in the past.

29.5 How to form: Negatives with "could"

To form negatives with **could**, put **not** after **could**. We often shorten **could not** to **couldn't**.

We could see the moon last night.

⬇

We could not see the moon last night.

Put **not** after **could**.

We often shorten **could not** to **couldn't**.

When to use
Use **could not** or **couldn't** to talk about things someone or something was unable to do in the past.

29.6 How to form: Questions with "could"

To ask questions with **could**, put **could** before the subject.

You could see the moon last night.

✗

Could you see the moon last night?

Put **could** before the subject, **you**.

When to use
Use questions with **could** to ask if someone or something was able to do something in the past.

Further examples

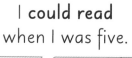
I **could read** when I was five.

He **could hear** the birds singing.

Maria **could understand** all the teacher's questions.

I **couldn't ride** my bike last week. It was broken.

We **couldn't visit** the museum yesterday because it was closed.

Andy **couldn't lift** the box because it was too heavy.

Could you swim when you were four?

Could Dad snowboard when he was a child?

Could you answer all the questions on the math test?

30 "May" for requests and permission

See also:
Modal verbs **28**
"Might," "may," and "could" **32**

Yes, you may.

May I have **an apple, please?**

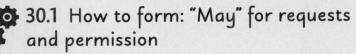

30.1 How to form: "May" for requests and permission

May is a modal verb. **May** stays the same for all subjects. To ask questions with **may**, put **may** before the subject.

May	subject	base form	rest of sentence
May	**I** / **we**	have	**an apple, please?**

We mostly use **I** or **we** to make a request or to ask for permission.

30.2 Using "may" for requests and permission

May I have **a pear, please?**

May stays the same for all subjects.

When to use
Use **may** to ask for something.

May **we play outside?**

May is followed by the main verb in its base form.

Use **may** to ask for permission to do something.

Further examples

May I buy a new toy?

May we play soccer?

May we go to the fair?

May we have some juice, please?

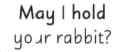

May I hold your rabbit?

May I eat a cookie?

May I have some ice cream?

May we visit Grandma again soon?

May I wear my new dress tonight?

31 "Must," "have to," and "have got to"

See also:
Present simple 01
Modal verbs 28

> I must go now, my dinner is ready.

31.1 How to form: "Must," "have to," and "have got to"

Must is a modal verb. Use **must** followed by a base form.
Must stays the same for all subjects. **Have to** becomes **has to**
and **have got to** becomes **has got to** for **he**, **she**, and **it**.

subject	must/have to/have got to	base form
I You	must have to have got to	go.
He She It	must has to has got to	go.
We You They	must have to have got to	go.

When to use
Use **must, have to,**
or **have got to** to talk
about things someone
needs to do.

Further examples

I **must wear** a coat because it's raining.

Andy **has to eat** all his vegetables.

I **have to get up** for school now.

Sofia **has got to clean** her room.

He **must finish** his letter before dinner.

She's **got to practice** her trumpet.

TIP!
In **have to** sentences, you can't shorten **have to** to 've to or **has to** to 's to.

We **must run** to catch the bus.

They **have to wear** a uniform to school.

31.2 How to form: Negatives with "must"

To form negatives with **must**, put **not** after **must**.

You **must** be **careful in science class.**

You **must not touch the fire.**

Put **not** after **must.**

When to use
Use **must not** when you are not allowed to do something.

TIP!
The negative forms of **must** and **have to/have got to** do not mean the same thing.

Further examples

You **must not drop** litter.

You **must not use** a calculator on the test.

You **must not swim** in the ocean today.

31.3 How to form: Negatives with "have to" and "have got to"

To form negatives with **have to**, put **do not** or **does not**
before **have** or **has**, but change **has** to its base form, **have**.
We often shorten **do not** to **don't** and **does not** to **doesn't**.

She **has to go** to school on Mondays.

⬇

She **does not** have to go **to school on the weekend.**

Put **do not** or
does not before
have or **has**.

To **have** is in ts base form.

To form negatives with **have got to**, put **not** after **have** or **has**.
We often shorten **have not** to **haven't** and **has not** to **hasn't**.

She **has got to walk** to school today.

⬇

She **has not got to walk** to school today.

Put **not** after **have** or **has**.

> **When to use**
> Use **do not have to** or
> **have not got to** when you
> don't need to do something
> or when you're allowed to
> do something, but
> it isn't necessary.

Further examples

Sofia **doesn't have to
leave** the party yet.

You **haven't got to go**
to bed yet.

We **don't have to sing**
in the concert. We could
play our guitars!

31.4 How to form: Questions with "have to" and "have got to"

We don't usually ask questions using **must**. To ask questions with **have to**, put **do** or **does** before the subject, and change **has** to its base form, **have**.

He **has to** go **to bed.**

Does he **have to** go **to bed?**

Use **do** for I, **you, we, you,** or **they.**
Use **does** for **he, she,** or **it.**

When to use
Use questions with **have to** or **have got to** to ask about things someone needs to do.

To ask questions with **have got to**, put **have** or **has** before the subject.

He **has got to** go **to bed.**

Has he **got to** go **to bed?**

Put **has** before the subject, **he.**

Further examples

Do I have to take a hat with me?

Does he have to stay at home today?

Do they have to wear a uniform to work?

31.5 How to form: Past form of "have to"

There is no past form of **must** or **have got to**. **Had to** is the past form of **have to**. Use **had to** followed by a base form. **Had to** stays the same for all subjects. Do not add an **s** for **he**, **she**, or **it**.

When to use
Use **had to** to talk about things someone needed to do in the past.

subject	had to	base form	rest of sentence
I	had to	clean	my cleats after soccer.

Had to stays the same for all subjects.

Further examples

I **had to get up** early yesterday.

He **had to answer** ten questions on the test.

They **had to paint** a picture today.

We **had to catch** a bus into town because my bike was broken.

They **had to whisper** in the library.

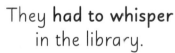

32 "Might," "may," and "could" for possibility

See also:
"Can" for ability **29**
"May" **30**

We might go to the fair today, but we're not sure.

32.1 How to form: "Might" and "may" for possibility

Might and **may** are modal verbs. Use **might** or **may** followed by a base form.
Might and **may** stay the same for all subjects. Do not add an **s** for **he**, **she**, or **it**.

subject	might/may	base form	rest of sentence
We	might / may	go	to the fair today.

Might and **may** mean the same thing.

When to use
Use **might** or **may** to talk about something that is possibly happening or going to happen, or something that is uncertain.

88

32.2 How to form: Negatives with "might" and "may"

To form negatives with **might** or **may**,
put **not** after **might** or **may**.

We **might go** to the fair today.

⬇

We **might not go** to the fair today.

Put **not** after **might** or **may**.

Further examples

The cat **may be** asleep.

They **might play** a board game later.

He **might not hit** the ball.

Andy **may not go** to school today because he is sick.

She **might paint** a picture of a house.

Look at those clouds. It **might rain**.

⚙ 32.3 How to form: "Could" for possibility

Could is a modal verb. Use **could** followed by a base form. **Could** stays the same for all subjects. Do not add an **s** for **he**, **she**, or **it**.

subject	could	base form	rest of sentence
It	**could**	**snow**	**today. It's very cold.**

Could stays the same for all subjects.

When to use
Use **could** to talk about things that have a chance of happening or being true. Its negative form can't be used in this context.

Further examples

Andy is very tired. He **could fall** asleep.

Don't drop that! It **could break**.

They're playing really well. They **could win** the game!

Be careful! You **could fall over**!

Cycling without a helmet **could be** dangerous.

33 "Could" for suggestions

See also:
Modal verbs **28**
"Can" for ability **29**

> You could play a game.

⚙ 33.1 How to form: "Could" for suggestions

Could is a modal verb. Use **could** followed by a base form. **Could** stays the same for all subjects. Do not add an **s** for **he**, **she**, or **it**.

When to use
Use **could** to make a suggestion. You can say **or** to give someone more than one option.

subject	could	base form	rest of sentence
You	**could**	**play**	**a game.**

Could stays the same for all subjects.

Further examples

Maria **could wear** her new shoes to Grandma's today.

It's a sunny day. We **could go** to the beach or the lake.

> You **could put on** a sweater.

> I'm cold!

34 "Should"

See also:
Modal verbs **28**
"Could" for suggestions **33**

It's windy today. You should wear a coat.

34.1 How to form: "Should"

Should is a modal verb. Use **should** followed by a base form. **Should** stays the same for all subjects. Do not add an **s** for **he, she,** or **it**.

subject	should	base form	rest of sentence
You	should	wear	a coat.

Should stays the same for all subjects.

When to use
Use **should** to offer or ask for advice.

34.2 How to form: Negatives and questions with "should"

To form negatives with **should**, put **not** after **should**. We often shorten **should not** to **shouldn't**.

You should go outside.

⬇

You should **not** go outside.

To ask questions with **should**, put **should** before the subject.

We should take an umbrella.

Should we take an umbrella?

Put **should** before the subject, **we.**

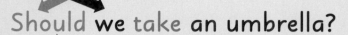

Further examples

It's 7 o'clock. Maria **should get up**.

The puppy **shouldn't eat** that!

Should we buy some cereal for our camping trip?

It's very hot today. You **should drink** lots of water.

Amy **shouldn't stay up** late. She has school tomorrow.

They **should go** camping in the summer when it's warm.

Should Sara bake a cake or some cookies?

You **should try** this cake. It's delicious!

35 "Would like"

See also:
Infinitives and base forms **42**
Nouns **50**

> I would like **some ice cream.**

> I would like **to go to the park.**

⚙ 35.1 How to form: "Would like"

Would is a modal verb. Add the base form of **like** to form **would like**.
Would like stays the same for all subjects. **Would like** can be followed
by a noun or an infinitive verb with **to**.

subject	would like	noun
I	would like	some ice cream.

When to use
Use **would like** with
a noun to politely
ask for something.

subject	would like	infinitive	rest of sentence
I	would like	to go	to the park.

When used with a verb, **would like**
is followed by an infinitive with **to**.

Use **would like** with
a verb to politely
say you want to
do something.

Further examples

Ben **would like**
to play a game.

I **would like** another
glass of juice, please.

He'd **like** to
read a book.

35.2 How to form: Questions with "would like"

To ask questions with **would like**, put **would** before the subject.

You would like **some ice cream.**

Would **you** like **some ice cream?**

⌐ Put **would** before the subject, **you**.

⌐ **Like** stays in the same position.

When to use
Use questions with **would like** and a noun to ask someone politely if they want something.

You would like **to go to the park.**

Would **you** like **to go to the park?**

Use questions with **would like** and an infinitive to ask someone politely if they want to do something.

Further examples

TIP!
You can shorten **would** to **'d**.

I would like ➡ I'd like

Go to R20 to find out more.

Would you like to play with me?

Would you like to draw a picture?

Would you like an apple?

Would you like some help with your homework?

36 Zero conditional

See also:
Present simple **1**
Imperatives **26**

When it snows,
we build a snowman.

⚙ 36.1 How to form: Zero conditional

To form the zero conditional, use **if** or **when** followed by an action or situation, then the result of that action or situation. Both parts are in the present simple.

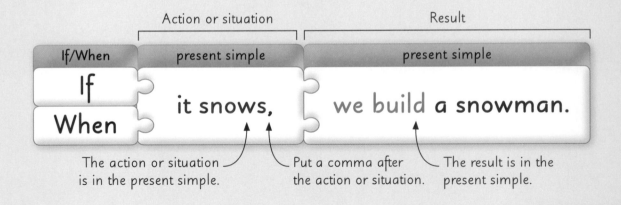

Action or situation

Result

If/When	present simple	present simple
If **When**	**it snows,**	**we build a snowman.**

The action or situation is in the present simple.

Put a comma after the action or situation.

The result is in the present simple.

You can form these sentences another way by moving the result before the action or situation. There is no comma when you form them this way.

When it snows, we build a snowman.

We build a snowman when it snows.

There is no comma.

When to use
Use the **zero condition**
to talk about somethin
that always happens
as a result of an action
or situation.

⚙ 36.2 How to form: Zero conditional with an imperative

You can also use the zero conditional followed by an imperative.

	Action or situation	Suggested action
If/When	**present simple**	**imperative**
If / **When**	**you're cold,**	wear **a warm coat.**

The action or situation is in the present simple.

The suggested action is an imperative.

When to use

Use the **zero conditional** with an **imperative** to tell someone what they should do if or when an action or situation happens.

TIP!
You can put the suggested action before the action or situation. There is no comma when you do this.

Further examples

I play with my toys if **I'm bored.**

When **it rains, we can't play** in the yard.

When **I'm tired, I go** to bed early.

When **the dog is hungry, give** it some food.

If **you're thirsty, drink** some water.

Go to the doctor if **you're ill.**

37 First conditional

See also:
Present simple **1**
"Will" **21**

> If we win the competition,
> we'll get a trophy.

 37.1 How to form: First conditional
To form the first conditional, say **if** followed by an action or situation in the present simple, then the result using **will**.

Likely action or situation | | Future result

If	present simple	will
If	**we win the competition,**	**we'll get a trophy.**

The action or situation is in the present simple.

Put a comma after the action or situation.

The result uses **will**.

REMEMBER!
We often shorten **will** to **'ll**.
Go to 21.3 to find out more.

You can form these sentences another way by moving the future result before the likely action or situation. There is no comma when you form them this way.

If we win the competition, we'll get a trophy.

We'll get a trophy if we win the competition.

There is no comma.

When to use
Use the **first conditional** to talk about the probable result of an action or situation that is likely to happen.

Further examples

If **I drop** this,
it will break.

You'll feel better if
you take this medicine.

If **I clean** my room,
Mom will be happy.

He'll fall off if
he's not careful.

If **it's sunny** tomorrow,
we'll go to the beach.

If **we get** a dog,
we'll walk it every day.

They'll win
the game if **he**
catches the ball!

38 Forming questions

See also:
Short answers **39**
Question words **40**

There are two ways to form questions in English:
put the verb before the subject or use **do**, **does**, or **did**.

38.1 How to form: Present simple questions

To ask questions in the present simple with verbs that aren't
to be or a modal verb, use **do** or **does** and put the main
verb in its base form. Do not add an **s** to the main verb.

She likes board games.

Does she like board games?

Add **do**
or **does**.

The main verb is
in its base form.

38.2 How to form: Past simple questions

To ask questions in the past simple with verbs that aren't **to be**,
use **did** and put the main verb in its base form. Do not use the
past simple form of the verb. **Did** stays the same for all subjects.

He played basketball.

Did he play basketball?

Put **did** at
the start of
the question.

The main verb is
in its base form.

38.3 How to form: Present simple questions with "to be"

To ask present simple questions with **to be**, put **am**, **is**, or **are** before the subject.

He is **tall.**

Is he **tall?**

Put **am**, **is**, or **are** before the subject.

38.4 How to form: Past simple questions with "to be"

To ask past simple questions with **to be**, put **was** or **were** before the subject.

It was **windy.**

Was it **windy?**

Put **was** or **were** before the subject.

38.5 How to form: Questions with modal verbs

To ask questions with modal verbs, put the modal verb before the subject. The main verb stays in the same position.

They can **sing well.**

Can they **sing well?**

Put the modal verb before the subject.

38.6 How to form: Questions in the present perfect

To ask questions in the present perfect, put **have** or **has** before the subject. The past participle stays in the same position.

She has **won.**

Has she **won?**

Put **have** or **has** before the subject.

39 Short answers

When you're answering questions, sometimes you can leave some words out.
This is called a short answer, and they're very common in spoken English.

 39.1 How to form: Short answers with "to be"

If a question starts with **to be**, use **to be** in the same tense in the short answer.

Are you **hungry**?

Yes, I am.

No, I'm not.

Further examples

Is it your tortoise?
Yes, **it is**.

Were you at school yesterday?
Yes, **we were**.

Was he studying English?
No, **he wasn't**.

 39.2 How to form: Short answers with "to do"

If a questions starts with **do**, **does**, or **did**, use the same form in the short answer.

Do you like burgers?

Yes, I do.

No, I don't.

Further examples

Do you like apples?
Yes, **I do**.

Does he wake up early?
No, **he doesn't**.

Did you win the game?
Yes, **we did**!

See also:
Modal verbs **28**
Forming questions **38**

⚙ 39.3 How to form: Short answers with "to have"

If a question starts with **have** or **has**, use the same form of **have** in the short answer.

Have you **read** this book?

Yes, I have.

No, I haven't.

⚙ 39.4 How to form: Short answers with modal verbs

If a question starts with a modal verb, use the same modal verb in the short answer.

Can you play the violin?

No, I can't.

Yes, I can.

Further examples

Has he bought a fish?
Yes, **he has**.

Have we got to leave?
Yes, **we have**.

Have they finished their dinner?
No, **they haven't**.

Further examples

Would you like a piece of cake?
Yes, **I would**.

Should she clean her boots?
Yes, **she should**.

May we watch TV?
No, **you may not**.

40 Question words

To ask questions that don't have a simple **yes** or **no** answer, we use question words.

See also:
Forming questions **38**

40.1 "Who"

Use **who** to ask questions about people.

Who is your best friend?

You are!

40.2 "Whose"

Use **whose** to ask who owns something.

Whose pencil is this?

It's mine.

40.3 "Where"

Use **where** to ask questions about places, directions, or the location of people or things.

Where is the library?

I'll show you.

40.4 "When"

Use **when** to ask questions about time.

When does the game start?

8 o'clock.

40.5 "What"

Use **what** to ask questions about things.

What are you doing?

I'm playing.

40.6 "Which"

Use **which** to ask someone to choose between two or more named things.

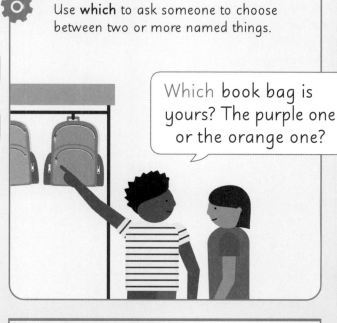

Which book bag is yours? The purple one or the orange one?

40.7 "What" and "which"

Use **what** to ask general questions about things. Use **which** when there are two or more options to choose from.

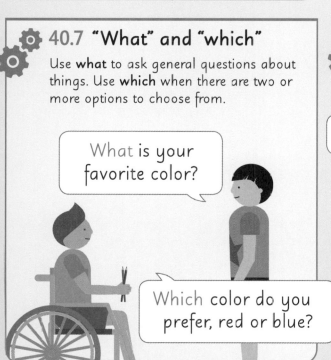

What is your favorite color?

Which color do you prefer, red or blue?

40.8 "Why"

Use **why** to ask for reasons.

Why are you crying?

I broke my skateboard.

40.9 "How"

Use **how** to ask for more details about something or to ask about the way something is done.

40.10 "How often"

Use **how often** to ask how many times someone does something.

40.11 "How many"

Use **how many** to ask questions about the quantity of countable nouns.

40.12 "How much"

Use **how much** to ask questions about the quantity of uncountable nouns.

Further examples

Who	Use to ask questions about people.	**Who** caught the ball? **Who** is winning the race?
Whose	Use to ask who owns something.	**Whose** jacket is this? **Whose** dog is named Spot?
Where	Use to ask about places, directions, or locations.	**Where** do you live? **Where** is she going?
When	Use to ask about time.	**When** do you get up in the morning? **When** are we going to go on vacation?
What	Use to ask about things.	**What** is your name? **What** is the time?
Which	Use to ask someone to choose between two or more things	**Which** do you prefer, cats or dogs? **Which** coat is yours?
Why	Use to ask for reasons.	**Why** is he laughing? **Why** are you late?
How	Use to ask for more details or how something is done.	**How** do you spell "kitchen"? **How** did you get to school?
How often	Use to ask many times someone does something.	**How often** do you play basketball? **How often** do they go to the beach?
How many	Use to ask about the quantity of countable nouns.	**How many** balloons are there? **How many** birds can you see?
How much	Use to ask about the quantity of uncountable nouns.	**How much** cake is there? **How much** juice would you like?

41 Tag questions

See also:
Modal verbs **28**
Forming questions **38**

> The gray dog is very big, isn't it?

TIP!
For statements with **I am**, the negative tag question is **aren't I?**

41.1 How to form: Tag questions

Tag questions are short questions added to the end of a statement. If the statement is positive, use a negative tag question.

positive statement	negative tag question
The gray dog is very big,	**isn't it?**

The verb is positive. — The tag question is negative.

If the statement is negative, use a positive tag question.

negative statement	positive tag question
The brown dog isn't very big,	**is it?**

The verb is negative. — The tag question is positive.

When to use

Use **tag questions** to invite someone to agree with you or to ask whether what you have just said is correct.

41.2 Using tag questions with "to be"

For sentences with **to be**, use **to be** in the tag question.

It is really hot today, isn't it?

The verb is **to be**. — The verb in the tag question is **to be**.

41.3 Using tag questions with other verbs

The type of tag question you use depends on the verb in the first part of the sentence.

For most verbs in the present simple, use **do**, **does**, **don't**, or **doesn't**.

You love dancing, don't you?

For most verbs in the past simple, use **did** or **didn't**

Ben played basketball today, didn't he?

For modal verbs, use the same modal verb in the tag question.

We shouldn't go outside, should we?

When **to have** is being used to make the present perfect or in phrases with **to have got to**, use **to have** in the tag question.

You haven't read this book, have you?

41.4 How to say: Tag questions

There are two ways to say tag questions. When the tag question needs an answer, your voice goes up at the end.

You are coming to my party, aren't you?

Your voice goes up.

When you're just asking someone to agree with you and the tag question doesn't need an answer, your voice goes down at the end.

Your voice goes down.

That game was really fun, wasn't it?

42 Infinitives and base forms

See also:
Gerunds 43
Verb patterns 44

42.1 Infinitives and base forms

Infinitives and base forms are the simplest forms of verbs in English. Infinitives always start with **to** and are sometimes called "to-infinitives." A verb's base form is always the same as its infinitive, but without **to**.

subject	verb	infinitive
I	like	to read.

Infinitives always start with **to**.

subject	verb	base form	rest of sentence
I	should	read	more books.

This is a base form. There is no **to**.

When to use
We don't use **infinitives** and **base forms** on their own very often, but we use them to make lots of different kinds of sentences.

Further examples

I need **to clean** my room.

Dad decided **to cook** pasta for dinner.

Sara can **ride** a bike.

We should **go** inside because we're too wet!

43 Gerunds

See also:
Infinitives and base forms **42**
Verb patterns **44**

43.1 Gerunds

A gerund is a verb that is acting as a noun.

Swimming is fun!

Here, **swimming** is a noun.

When to use
Use **gerunds** to say how you feel about an activity.

Further examples

Eating fruits and vegetables is important.

Skiing is exciting!

I love **baking**. It's my favorite hobby.

43.2 Spelling rules: Gerunds

To form gerunds, add **ing** to the base form of the verb.

wear
⬇
wear**ing**

Add **ing** to most verbs.

Sometimes, the spelling of the base form changes a little before we add **ing**.

Last letter is a silent **e**.

choose
⬇
choos**ing**

Take away the **e**, then add **ing**.

Last letters are **ie**.

tie
⬇
ty**ing**

Change **ie** to **y**, then add **ing**.

Final syllable is stressed and last letters are consonant, vowel, consonant.

forget
⬇
forget**ting**

Write the last letter twice, unless it's **w**, **x**, or **y**, then add **ing**.

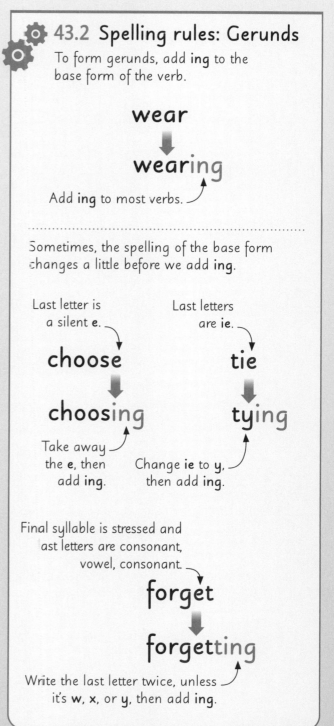

44 Verb patterns

See also:
Infinitives and base forms 42
Gerunds 43

44.1 How to form: Verb patterns with infinitives and gerunds

A verb can be followed by a second verb. Some verbs can only be followed by an infinitive or a gerund. Other verbs can be followed by either with no difference in meaning.

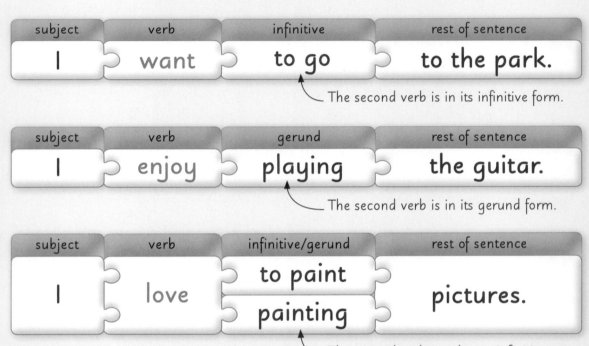

subject	verb	infinitive	rest of sentence
I	want	to go	to the park.

The second verb is in its infinitive form.

subject	verb	gerund	rest of sentence
I	enjoy	playing	the guitar.

The second verb is in its gerund form.

subject	verb	infinitive/gerund	rest of sentence
I	love	to paint / painting	pictures.

The second verb can be an infinitive or a gerund. They mean the same thing here.

44.2 Verbs followed by an infinitive, a gerund, or either

Verb + infinitive		Verb + gerund		Verb + infinitive or gerund	
agree	help	complete	keep	begin	love
ask	hope	dislike	miss	continue	prefer
choose	learn	enjoy	practice	hate	start
decide	want	finish	understand	like	

44.3 How to form: Verb patterns with objects

When the verb **to have** is followed by an infinitive, you can put an object between **to have** and the infinitive.

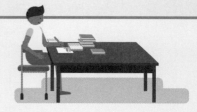

subject	have/has	object	infinitive
I	have	a story	to write.

When to use
Use this **verb pattern** to talk about things that you can do or that you need to do.

Further examples

She **is learning to spell**.

Max **decided to buy** a blue ball.

Ben **likes to play** with his car.

Maria **has finished eating** her dinner.

They **practice speaking** English every day.

Sara **likes riding** her bike.

Sofia **has two** bags **to carry**.

We **have a bus to catch**.

I **have ten questions to answer**.

⚙ 45.1 Indefinite articles

A, **an**, and **some** are indefinite articles.

I'd like a pear.

Use **a** in front of singular nouns starting with a consonant.

When to use

Use **indefinite articles** to talk about things in general or to talk about something for the first time.

I'd like an apple.

Use **an** in front of singular nouns starting with a vowel.

I'd like some mangoes.

Use **some** in front of plural or uncountable nouns.

⚙ 45.2 "Any" with questions and negatives

In questions and negative sentences, the indefinite article **some** becomes **any**.

There are some bananas.
⬇
Are there any bananas?

There are some bananas.
⬇
There aren't any bananas.

Further examples

That's **a** nice drawing.

My dad is **an** actor.

Look! There's **a** spider!

There aren't **any** cookies in the jar.

There is **some** milk in the fridge.

We need **some** flour for this cake.

Would you like **an** orange?

Do you have **any** pens?

45.3 The definite article

The is called the definite article.

I'm in the yard.

The yard is a specific place, so we use **the**.

When to use
Use **the** to talk about a specific thing or place.

Use the indefinite article to talk about something for the first time.

We have a dog, a rabbit, and a tortoise. The dog is named Rex.

Use **the** because the dog has already been talked about.

Use **the** to talk about something that's already been mentioned.

Rex is the biggest.

Use **the** before a superlative.

Use **the** before a superlative adjective or adverb.

Further examples

Max is **the** fastest in our school.

We are washing **the** car.

I loved **the** clown at Maria's party.

I can see a butterfly and a ladybug. **The** butterfly is blue.

⚙ 45.4 Comparing indefinite and definite articles

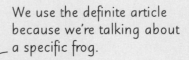

We use the definite article because we're talking about a specific frog.

My favorite animal is a frog.

We use the indefinite article because we're talking about frogs in general.

The frog in our yard is green.

When to use
Use the **indefinite article** to talk about something in general. Use the **definite article** to talk about something specific.

Further examples

Maria would like **a** cookie.

The cookies at the party were delicious!

I'm going to buy **a** new toy car.

The toy car in the store is expensive.

⚙ 46.1 Demonstrative determiners

This, **that**, **these**, and **those** can come before a noun to specify which thing or things you are talking about. When they do this, they are demonstrative determiners.

This robot is green.

When to use
Use **this** before a singular or uncountable noun that is nearby.

That robot is red.

Use **that** before a singular or uncountable noun that is far away.

These robots are green.

Use **these** before a plural noun that is nearby.

Those robots are red.

Use **those** before a plural noun that is far away.

See also:
Nouns **50**
Possessive adjectives **55**

Further examples

I love **this** dress!

This music is great.

This pear is delicious.

Ben would like to use **that** computer.

That elephant is very big!

That game looks fun.

Have you tried **these** cupcakes?

I've read all **these** books.

These flowers smell lovely.

Those children are playing in the park.

Can you see **those** lions?

Look at **those** kites!

⚙ 46.2 Demonstrative pronouns

This, **that**, **these**, and **those** can also replace a noun in a sentence.
When they do this, they are demonstrative pronouns.

This **is my cat.**

This cat **is my cat.**

This **is my cat.**

When to use
Use **this** to replace a singular or uncountable noun that is nearby.

That **is your cat.**

We often shorten **that is** to **that's**.

Use **that** to replace a singular or uncountable noun that is far away.

These **are my cats.**

Use **these** to replace a plural noun that is nearby.

Those **are your cats.**

Use **those** to replace a plural noun that is far away.

Further examples

This tastes great!

Is **this** your sweater?

Can you hold **this** for me, please?

That is a nice book bag.

That's a very cute dog.

I think **that**'s broken.

These are my dolls.

These are my new sneakers.

Are **these** your pencils?

Those are the sandwiches for my party.

Those are my paintings.

Are **those** for me?

47 "Another"

See also:
"Both" 48
Numbers 61

May I have another apple, please?

 47.1 "Another"

You can use **another** before a singular noun or a plural noun with a number.

May I have another apple, please?

Use **another** before a singular noun.

One or a different number can replace the noun.

May I have another apple, please?

May I have another one, please?

You can replace the noun with the word **one** or a different number.

When to use
Use **another** to talk about more of something or a different version of something.

Further examples

I'd like **another two pears**, please.

I've finished my drink. May I have **another one**, please?

Maria wants to borrow **another** book.

48 "Both"

See also:
"Another" 47

Are you having fries or salad?

I'm having both.

⚙ 48.1 "Both"

I'm having both.

This means Max asked for fries and salad.

> **When to use**
> Use **both** to talk about two people or things together. You can use **both** on its own; before two nouns or a plural noun; or after **we, us, they,** or **them.**

Both of them are having salad.

⌐ This means Max and Andy are having salad.

> Use **both of** to talk about two people or things together. You can use **both of** before **us, you,** or **them** or before a plural noun that has **the, these,** or **those** before it.

Both of the boys are having salad.

⌐ You can use **both of** before a plural noun that has **the, these,** or **those** before it.

Further examples

I like **both** sweaters.

They **both** love playing tennis.

Both of us enjoy singing.

123

See also:
Nouns 50

> I've tried every flavor of ice cream in this store.

49.1 "Each" and "every"

Each and every often mean the same thing. Use them before a singular noun.

I've tried | **each** / **every** | flavor.

In this sentence, **each** and **every** mean the same thing.

When to use
Use **each** and **every** to talk about a whole collection of things at once.

Further examples

Each dog has a toy.

Every player is wearing a red T-shirt.

Each flower in the vase is pink.

49.2 "Each"

Sometimes, **each** has a slightly different meaning to **every**.

Andy filled each glass with juice.

When to use
Use **each** to talk about single things in a group or small numbers of things.

49.3 "Every"

Sometimes, **every** has a slightly different meaning to **each**.

I go swimming every Sunday.

When to use
Use **every** to talk about a whole group of something; large numbers; or times like days, months, seasons, or years.

Further examples

Each cat is a different color.

Paint **each** shape blue.

Further examples

We go skiing **every** winter.

I've read **every** book on my bookshelf.

50 Nouns

See also:
Articles **45**
Quantity **62**

50.1 Common nouns

Nouns are "naming" words. Nouns in English do not have a gender.
Common nouns are words for everyday objects, animals, seasons, and actions.

house

baby

armchair

smile

farmer

spring

lunch

castle

giraffe

doll

50.2 Proper nouns

Proper nouns are words for specific people, places, days,
and months. Proper nouns always start with a capital letter.

Mount Everest

Italy

Paris

Mon
Monday

Nov
November

Max

Maria

Texas

Lake Victoria

Central Park

50.3 Singular and plural nouns

Nouns can be singular or plural. A singular noun refers to one thing. A plural noun refers to two or more things. To make most nouns plural, add an **s** to a singular noun.

drink

drink**s**

Add an **s** to a singular noun.

Irregular plural nouns

Add **es** to nouns that end with **s**, **x**, **z**, **ch**, or **sh**.

class → clas**ses**

box → bo**xes**

quiz → qui**zzes**

watch → wat**ches**

dish → di**shes**

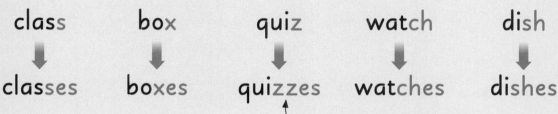

If the noun ends with one **z**, add another **z** before **es**.

Add **es** to most nouns that end with **o**. If there's another vowel before the **o**, just add **s**.

potato → potat**oes**

radio → radi**os**

Some nouns are completely irregular. Go to R26 for a list of irregular plural nouns.

child → child**ren**

person → people

For nouns that end with a consonant and then **y**, change the **y** to an **i**, then add **es**.

dictionary → dictiona**ries**

story → sto**ries**

Some nouns stay the same when they are plural.

fish → fish

sheep → sheep

50.4 Countable and uncountable nouns

Nouns that can be individually counted are called countable nouns.
Nouns that cannot be counted are called uncountable nouns.

Countable nouns

Use **a**, **an**, **some**, **any**, or a number in front of countable nouns.

I need a lemon for the cake.

This is a countable noun. You can
count how many lemons there are.

I need three lemons for the cake.

This is a countable noun. You can
count how many lemons there are.

I need some lemons for the cake.

Some means that there is an unspecified number
of lemons, but definitely more than one.

Do we need any lemons for the cake?

In negative sentences and questions, **some**
becomes **any**. Go to 45.2 to find out more.

Uncountable nouns

Use **some** or **any** in front of uncountable nouns.

I need some flour for the cake.

This is an uncountable noun.
You cannot count flour.

Is there any flour for the cake?

In negative sentences
and questions, **some**
becomes **any**. Go to
45.2 to find out more.

50.5 "How many" and "how much"

Use **how many** with countable nouns to ask what number of things there are.

How many oranges **do you need?**

Use **how many** with countable nouns.

Use **how much** with uncountable nouns to ask what amount of something there is.

How much rice **is there?**

Use **how much** with uncountable nouns.

Further examples

My dad bought **a car** today.

There's **some sand** in my shoe.

There are **five balloons.**

How many apples would you like?

How much sugar do we need?

51 Personal subject pronouns

See also:
Personal object pronouns 52
Reflexive pronouns 53

This is Maria. She likes books.

 51.1 How to form: Personal subject pronouns

Personal subject pronouns replace the subject of a sentence.

This is Maria. **Maria** likes books.

Maria is the subject of the sentence.

This is Maria. **She** likes books.

She is a personal subject pronoun. **She** replaces Maria's name.

I / You	like	
He / She / It	likes	books.
We / You / They	like	

The pronoun you use depends on who you are talking about.

When to use
Use **personal subject pronouns** to talk about the subject of a sentence. They often replace someone's name.

TIP!
There are no polite or familiar forms of **you** in English. **You** is also the same if you are talking to one person or more than one person.

51.2 Using personal subject pronouns

I'm ten years old today.

Use **I** to talk about yourself. It is always a capital letter

You play the trumpet very well.

Use **you** when you talk directly to one person.

He is on the playground.

Use **he** to talk about a boy or a man.

She is doing her homework.

Use **she** to talk about a girl or a woman.

It has a yellow ball.

Use **it** to talk about things or animals.

We are having fun at the beach.

Use **we** to talk about a group of at least two people that includes yourself.

You are happy!

Use **you** when you talk directly to more than one person

They are playing baseball.

Use **they** to talk about a group of people, animals, or things.

52 Personal object pronouns

See also:
Personal subject pronouns **51**
Reflexive pronouns **53**

> The car is dirty, so we're washing it.

⚙ 52.1 How to form: Personal object pronouns

Personal object pronouns replace the object of a sentence.

The car is dirty, so we're washing the car.

The car is dirty, so we're washing it.

The car is the object of the sentence.

It is a personal object pronoun. It replaces **the car**.

When to use
Use **personal object pronouns** when you or other people or things are the object of a sentence. They often replace someone's name.

TIP!
You is the same if you are talking to one person or more than one person.

I	you	he	she	it	we	you	they	subject pronouns
↓	↓	↓	↓	↓	↓	↓	↓	
me	you	him	her	it	us	you	them	object pronouns

52.2 Using personal object pronouns

Do you want to play a game with me?

Use **me** to talk about yourself.

I saw you at the park yesterday.

Use **you** when you talk to one person directly.

My brother was bored, so I'm reading him a story.

Use **him** to talk about a boy or a man.

It's Sara's birthday, so I am giving her a present.

Use **her** to talk about a girl or a woman.

Mia lost her pencil and I found it.

Use **it** to talk about things or animals.

Dad gave us some money.

Use **us** to talk about a group of at least two people that includes yourself.

May I take a picture of you?

Use **you** when you talk to more than one person directly.

I play basketball with them.

Use **them** to talk about a group of people, animals, or things.

53 Reflexive pronouns

See also:
Personal subject pronouns **51**
Personal object pronouns **52**

> I am drawing myself.

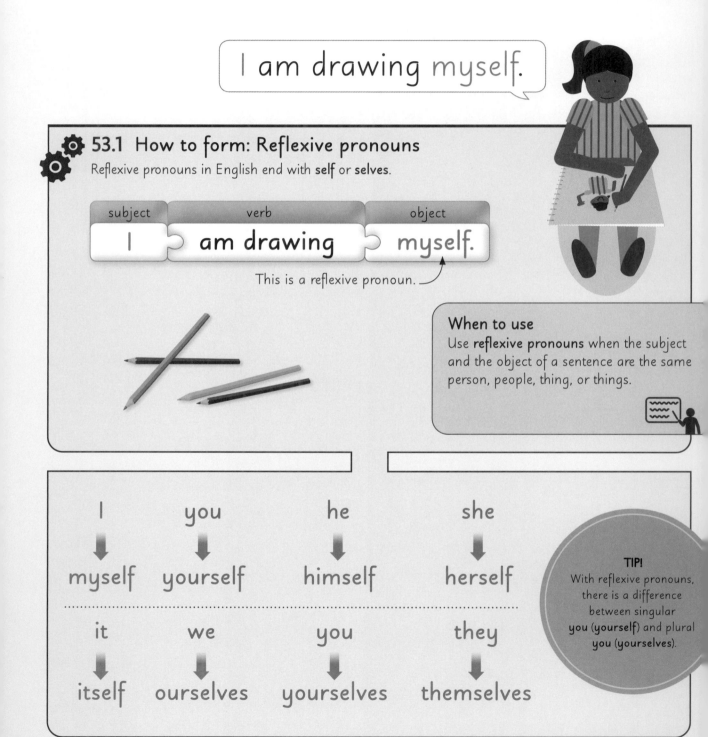

53.1 How to form: Reflexive pronouns

Reflexive pronouns in English end with **self** or **selves**.

subject	verb	object
I	am drawing	myself.

This is a reflexive pronoun.

When to use
Use **reflexive pronouns** when the subject and the object of a sentence are the same person, people, thing, or things.

I	you	he	she
↓	↓	↓	↓
myself	yourself	himself	herself

it	we	you	they
↓	↓	↓	↓
itself	ourselves	yourselves	themselves

TIP!
With reflexive pronouns, there is a difference between singular **you** (yourself) and plural **you** (yourselves).

53.2 Using reflexive pronouns

I bought **myself** a new toy with my birthday money.

When the subject is I, use **myself**.

Oh no! You've hurt **yourself**.

When the subject is **you** for one person, use **yourself**.

Andy is teaching **himself** the guitar.

When the subject is **he** or a boy or man's name, use **himself**.

She has made **herself** a sandwich.

When the subject is **she** or a girl or woman's name, use **herself**.

Look at the cat. It's licking **itself**.

When the subject is **it**, use **itself**.

We are taking a picture of **ourselves**.

When the subject is **we**, use **ourselves**.

Can you see **yourselves** in the mirror?

When the subject is **you** for more than one person, use **yourselves**.

They are enjoying **themselves**.

When the subject is **they** or more than one person's name, use **themselves**.

54 Indefinite pronouns

Indefinite pronouns are words that we use to talk about an unspecified person or thing.

54.1 "Someone"

Use **someone** to talk about an unspecified person in a positive sentence or a question.

Someone has lost their ruler.

54.2 "Anyone"

Use **anyone** to talk about no people in a negative sentence or an unspecified person in a positive sentence or a question.

There isn't anyone on the playground.

Further examples

Someone called when we were eating dinner.

Is **someone** knocking at the door?

I saw **someone** I know at the park.

Further examples

There isn't **anyone** on the stage.

Does **anyone** want to play tennis with me?

Does **anyone** want some juice?

See also:
Forming questions **38**

⚙ 54.3 "Everyone"

Use **everyone** to talk about a whole group of people in a positive sentence or a question.

Everyone in our school wears a uniform.

⚙ 54.4 "No one"

Use **no one** to talk about no people in a positive sentence.

No one is allowed to wear sneakers.

Further examples

I invited **everyone** in my class to my birthday party.

The teacher asked **everyone** to be quiet.

Is **everyone** having fun?

Further examples

There was **no one** at the bus stop.

No one knew the answer to the question.

There's **no one** in the yard.

137

54.5 "Something"

Use **something** to talk about an unspecified or unnamed thing in a positive sentence or a question.

I've bought something for Maria's birthday.

Further examples

Sofia can see **something** in the box. What is it?

There's **something** in this bag. It's a surprise!

May I have **something** to eat, please?

54.6 "Anything"

Use **anything** to talk about an unspecified or unnamed thing in a positive sentence, a negative sentence, or a question.

I haven't bought anything.

Further examples

Ben is a great artist. He can draw **anything**.

It's so dark. I can't see **anything**!

Would you like **anything** to drink?

54.7 "Everything"

Use **everything** to talk about an entire group of things in a positive sentence, a negative sentence, or a question.

I'm going to eat everything on my plate.

Further examples

Andy likes **everything** in this toy store.

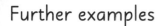

Have we got **everything** we need to bake a cake?

I can't carry **everything**!

54.8 "Nothing"

Use **nothing** when there isn't anything present. Use it in a positive sentence. In a negative sentence and most questions, use **anything** instead.

There's nothing left on my plate.

Further examples

My room is really clean. There's **nothing** on the floor!

I'm bored. There's **nothing** to do!

There's **nothing** in this bag. It's empty.

55 Possessive adjectives

See also:
Possessive pronouns **56**
Possessive apostrophes **57**

> Poppy is my cat.

> George is her cat.

⚙ 55.1 Possessive adjectives

Use possessive adjectives before a noun. The possessive adjective changes form depending on whether the owner is singular, plural, male, or female.

subject + verb	possessive adjective	noun
Poppy is	my	cat.

This means that the cat belongs to me.

Poppy is	your his her its our your their	cat.

When to use
Use **possessive adjectives** before a noun to show who it belongs to or before a family member. The possessive adjective you use depends on who the owner is, not the noun.

There are no polite or familiar forms of **your.** **Your** is also the same if you are talking to one person or more than one person.

55.2 Using possessive adjectives

This is **my** brother, Tom.

Use **my** to talk about something that belongs to you.

Here are **your** presents, Ben!

Use **your** to talk about something that belongs to the person you are talking to.

It's **his** birthday today.

Use **his** to talk about something that belongs to a boy or a man.

This is **her** bag.

Use **her** to talk about something that belongs to a girl or a woman.

The dog is playing with **its** ball.

Use **its** to talk about something that belongs to an animal or an object.

This is **our** new computer.

Use **our** to talk about something that belongs to a group of at least two people that includes yourself.

Is this **your** puppy?

Use **your** to talk about something that belongs to the people you are talking to.

They are playing with **their** toys.

Use **their** to talk about something that belongs to a group of people or things.

56 Possessive pronouns

See also:
Possessive adjectives 55
Possessive apostrophes 57

56.1 How to form: Possessive pronouns

Possessive pronouns replace a singular or
plural noun and tell you who it belongs to.

This rocket is my rocket.

This rocket is mine.   Mine replaces my rocket.

This rocket is	mine.
	yours.
	his. hers.
	ours. yours. theirs.

When to use
Use **possessive pronouns** to talk about
something someone owns. The
possessive pronoun you use depends
on who the owner is, not what the
noun is. There is no possessive
pronoun for **it**.

There are no polite or familiar
forms of **yours**. **Yours** is also the
same when you're talking to one
person or more than one person.

my	your	his	her	our	your	their	possessive adjectives
mine	yours	his	hers	ours	yours	theirs	possessive pronouns

56.2 Using possessive pronouns

Your robot is bigger than mine.

Use **mine** to talk about something that belongs to you.

Is this kite yours?

Use **yours** to talk about something that belongs to the person you are talking to.

That burger is his.

Use **his** to talk about something that belongs to a boy or a man.

My dress is green and hers is red.

Use **hers** to talk about something that belongs to a girl or a woman.

These toys are ours.

Use **ours** to talk about something that belongs to a group of at least two people that includes yourself.

Is that cat yours?

Use **yours** to talk about something that belongs to the people you are talking to.

That house is theirs.

Use **theirs** to talk about something that belongs to two or more people.

57 Possessive apostrophes

> That is Ben's house.

 57.1 How to form: Possessive apostrophes

To show that someone or something owns something, add **'s** or sometimes just **'** after a noun or someone's name.

That is the house of Ben.

That is Ben's house.

For most names or singular nouns, add **'s**.

James's house

James' house

For names or singular nouns that end with an **s**, add **'s** or just **'**.

When to use
Use **possessive apostrophes** to show possession.

My grandparents' house

For plural nouns that end with an **s**, just add **'**.

The children's house

For plural nouns that don't end with an **s**, add **'s**.

See also:
Possessive adjectives **55**
Possessive pronouns **56**

Further examples

Chris' hair is black.

This is Maria**'s** cat.

Amy**'s** dad is
very tall.

Thomas**'s** dog
is small.

The men**'s** T-shirts
are green.

The doll**'s** dress
is pink.

Have you seen
Andy**'s** bag?

This is my
parents**'** car.

58 Relative pronouns

See also:
Clauses R6

Use the relative pronouns **who**, **that**, **which**, and **where** to introduce relative clauses. Relative clauses give more information about something you've already mentioned in the main clause.

58.1 "who" and "that"

This is my friend. He likes robots.

⬇

relative pronoun

This is my friend 〔 who / that 〕 likes robots.

Main clause ⤴   ⤴ Relative clause

When to use
Use **who** or **that** to introduce relative clauses about people

58.2 "which" and "that"

Ben drew a picture. It was very nice.

⬇

relative pronoun

Ben drew a picture 〔 which / that 〕 was very nice.

Main clause ⤴   ⤴ Relative clause

When to use
Use **which** or **that** to introduce relative clauses about things

58.3 "where"

This is the field. We play baseball here.

⬇

relative pronoun

This is the field 〔 where 〕 we play baseball.

Main clause ⤴   ⤴ Relative clause

When to use
Use **where** to introduce relative clauses about places

It's my brother **that** plays soccer, not me.

Further examples

I have a sister **who** is a doctor.

This is my cousin **who** speaks English.

I bought a new toy **which** I love.

This is the present **that** Andy gave me.

She read a book **that** was really interesting.

The street **where** I live is called Main Street.

This is the cafe **where** we met Sofia.

This is the pool **where** they swim on Saturdays.

59 "There is" and "there are"

See also:
Nouns **50**
"There was" and "there were" **60**

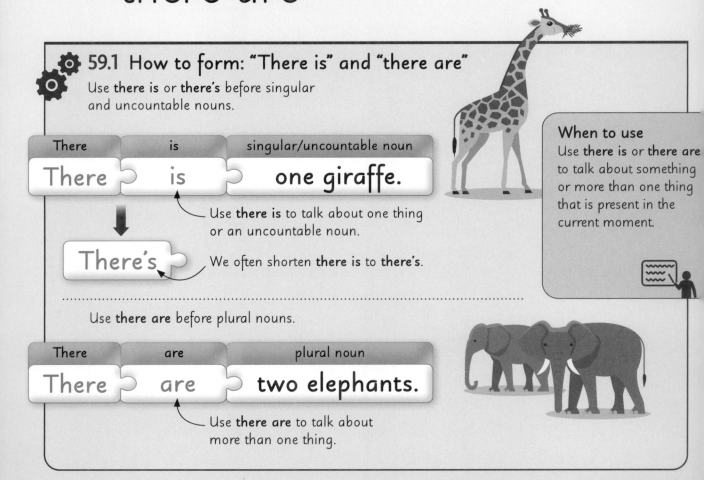

⚙ 59.1 How to form: "There is" and "there are"

Use **there is** or **there's** before singular and uncountable nouns.

There	is	singular/uncountable noun
There	is	**one giraffe.**

Use **there is** to talk about one thing or an uncountable noun.

There's — We often shorten **there is** to **there's**.

When to use
Use **there is** or **there are** to talk about something or more than one thing that is present in the current moment.

Use **there are** before plural nouns.

There	are	plural noun
There	are	**two elephants.**

Use **there are** to talk about more than one thing.

There's **one giraffe.**

There are **two elephants.**

Further examples

There's a kite.

There is one orange flower.

There are eight stars in the sky.

There are some cows in the field.

There's a book bag on the floor.

There is some rice on my plate.

There are two ants.

There's some fruit in the bowl.

There are four cars.

⚙ 59.2 How to form: Negatives with "there is" and "there are"

To form negatives with **there is** and **there are**, put **not** after **is** or **are**.
Use **there is not** before singular or uncountable nouns.

There is **a hippo.**

⬇

There is **not** a hippo.

⬇

There is**n't** a hippo.

....

Use **there are not** before plural nouns.

There are **some lions.**

⬇

There are **not any** lions.

⬇

There are**n't any** lions.

└ **Some** becomes **any.** Go to 45.2 to find out more.

When to use
Use **there is** or **there are** negatives to talk about something or more than one thing that is not present in the current moment.

Further examples

There isn't any honey left.

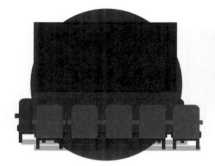

There aren't any people in the movie theater.

There isn't any food in the cupboard.

59.3 How to form: Questions with "there is" and "there are"

To form questions with **there is** and **there are**, put **is** or **are** before **there**.
Use **is there** before singular or uncountable nouns.

There is **a crocodile.**

Is there **a crocodile?**

⌐ Put **is** before **there**.

When to use
Use questions with
there is or **there are**
to ask if something
or more than one
thing is present in
the current moment.

....

Use **are there** before plural nouns.

There are **some lizards.**

Are there **any lizards?**

⌐ Put **are**   ⌐ **Some** becomes **any**.
before **there**.   Go to 45.2 to find out more.

Further examples

Is there a train
station in your town?

Are there any toys
in your room?

Is there any milk
in the pitcher?

There was a clown at the party.

There were balloons.

60.1 How to form: "There was" and "there were"

Use **there was** before singular or uncountable nouns.

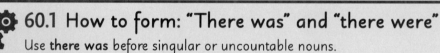

There	was	singular/uncountable noun
There	was	a clown.

Use **there was** to talk about one thing or an uncountable noun.

When to use
Use **there was** or **there were** to talk about something or more than one thing that was present in the past.

Use **there were** before plural nouns.

There	were	plural noun
There	were	balloons.

Use **there were** to talk about more than one thing.

Further examples

There were two giraffes.

There were lots of books in the library.

There was one cookie in the jar.

There was a bird in the tree.

There was some chocolate on the table.

There was a competition at school today.

There were three ducks in the water.

There were dolphins in the ocean.

There were some children at the park.

⚙ 60.2 How to form: Negatives with "there was" and "there were"

To form negatives with **there was** and **there were**, put **not** after **was** or **were**.
Use **there was not** before singular or uncountable nouns.

There was **a cake at the party.**

⬇

There was **not a cake at the party.**

⬇

There was**n't a cake at the party.**

Use **there were not** before plural nouns.

There were **some games at the party.**

⬇

There were **not any games at the party.**

⬇

There were**n't any games at the party.**

└ **Some** becomes **any**. Go to 45.2 to find out more.

When to use
Use **there was** or **there were** negatives to talk about something or more than one thing that was not present in the past.

Further examples

There weren't any teddy bears in the toy store.

There wasn't an elevator, so I used the stairs.

There wasn't any grass in the yard.

60.3 How to form: Questions with "there was" and "there were"

To form questions with **there was** and **there were**, put **was** or **were** before **there**. Use **was there** before singular or uncountable nouns.

There was **music.**

Was there **music?**

Put **was** before **there.**

When to use
Use questions with **there was** or **there were** to ask if something or more than one thing was present in the past.

Use **were there** before plural nouns.

There were **presents.**

Were there **presents?**

Put **were** before **there.**

Further examples

Was there a swimming pool at your hotel?

Were there lots of people at the beach?

Was there any juice at the store?

61 Numbers

We use numbers to count and to say how many of something there are.

See also:
Quantity 62
Syllables R4

61.1 Numbers

0 zero	**1** one	**2** two	**3** three	**4** four	**5** five
6 six	**7** seven	**8** eight	**9** nine	**10** ten	**11** eleven
12 twelve	**13** thirteen	**14** fourteen	**15** fifteen	**16** sixteen	**17** seventeen
18 eighteen	**19** nineteen	**20** twenty	**21** twenty-one	**22** twenty-two	**23** twenty-three
24 twenty-four	**25** twenty-five	**26** twenty-six	**27** twenty-seven	**28** twenty-eight	**29** twenty-nine
30 thirty	**40** forty	**50** fifty	**60** sixty	**70** seventy	**80** eighty
90 ninety	**100** one hundred	**101** one hundred one	**200** two hundred	**300** three hundred	**400** four hundred
500 five hundred	**600** six hundred	**700** seven hundred	**800** eight hundred	**900** nine hundred	**1000** one thousand

61.2 Numbers that sound similar

These numbers sound very similar. Make sure you stress the correct syllable to avoid confusion.

Stress the first syllable.

13	thir<u>teen</u>	30	<u>thir</u>ty
14	four<u>teen</u>	40	<u>for</u>ty
15	fif<u>teen</u>	50	<u>fif</u>ty
16	six<u>teen</u>	60	<u>six</u>ty
17	seven<u>teen</u>	70	<u>seven</u>ty
18	eigh<u>teen</u>	80	<u>eigh</u>ty
19	nine<u>teen</u>	90	<u>nine</u>ty

Stress the last syllable.

61.3 Ordinal numbers

We use ordinal numbers to count what position something is in a list.

1st first	2nd second	3rd third	4th fourth	5th fifth	6th sixth	7th seventh
8th eighth	9th ninth	10th tenth	11th eleventh	12th twelfth	13th thirteenth	
14th fourteenth	15th fifteenth	16th sixteenth	17th seventeenth	18th eighteenth	19th nineteenth	
20th twentieth	21st twenty-first	22nd twenty-second	23rd twenty-third	24th twenty-fourth	25th twenty-fifth	
26th twenty-sixth	27th twenty-seventh	28th twenty-eighth	29th twenty-ninth	30th thirtieth	31st thirty-first	

62 Quantity

English has several words to talk about how many or how much of something there is.

See also:
Articles **45**
Nouns **50**

62.1 Quantity words

There are some houses near the cafe.

When to use
Use **some** before plural or uncountable nouns to talk about an unspecific number or amount of something.

There are a few ducks in the pond.

Use **a few** before plural nouns to talk about a small number of things.

I saw lots of butterflies in the garden.

Use **lots of** or **a lot of** before plural or uncountable nouns to talk about a large number or amount of something.

There's enough flour to make this cake.

Use **enough** before plural or uncountable nouns when you have the number or amount of something that you need.

There are too many lemons!

Use **too many** before plural nouns when you have more things than you need.

There's too much sugar in the bowl.

Use **too much** before uncountable nouns when you have more of something than you need.

There's a little honey, but we need more.

Use **a little** or **a little bit of** before uncountable nouns when there's a small amount of something.

Further examples

There are **some** stars in the sky.

A few children were late to school today.

There are **lots of** birds in the yard.

I painted **a lot of** pictures today.

We have **enough** apples for the picnic.

There are **too many** toys on the floor.

I have **too much** rice in my bowl.

May I have **a little bit of** cake, please?

There's **a little** milk left.

63 Adjectives

See also:
Nouns 50
Intensifiers 71

63.1 Using adjectives

a **dirty** dog

a **wet** dog

a **big** dog

a **small** dog

63.2 How to form: Adjectives

In English, adjectives usually come before the noun. They stay the same when describing singular nouns and plural nouns.

When to use
Use **adjectives** to describe a noun.

start of sentence	adjective	singular noun
It is a	small	dog.

The adjective comes before the noun.

start of sentence	adjective	plural noun
They are	small	dogs.

The adjective stays the same for a plural noun.

Adjectives can come after the noun when they follow some verbs like **to be**.

subject	to be	adjective
The dog	is	small.

The adjective comes after the verb **to be**.

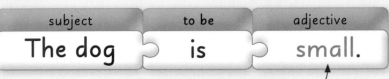

Further examples

I love **funny** movies.

I have a
new robot.

The clown was
very **silly**.

I like your **blue**
book bag.

Andy's wearing
a **purple** T-shirt.

My dogs are
friendly.

REMEMBER!
You can say **very** or
really before an adjective
to make it stronger.
Go to **71.1** to
find out more.

We're really **happy**.

It's very **windy** today.

I am tall. Sofia is taller.

64.1 How to form: Comparative adjectives

To form comparative adjectives for most one-syllable adjectives and some two-syllable adjectives, add **er** to the adjective.

subject	verb	comparative adjective
Sofia	is	taller.

Add **er** to the adjective, **tall**.

When to use
Use **comparative adjectives** to compare two or more things.

If you're comparing something to something else, say **than** after the comparative adjective.

subject	verb	comparative adjective	than	rest of sentence
Sofia	is	taller	than	Andy.

Say **than** after the comparative adjective.

64.2 Spelling rules: Comparative adjectives

To form these comparative adjectives, add **er** to the adjective. Sometimes, the spelling of the adjective changes before we add **er**.

Adjective ends consonant, vowel, consonant.

tall
⬇
taller
Add **er**.

close
⬇
closer
Just add **r**.

early
⬇
earlier
Change the **y** to an **i**, then add **er**.

big
⬇
bigger
Write the last letter twice, then add **er**.

See also:
Adjectives **63**
Syllables **R4**

 ## 64.3 How to form: Irregular comparative adjectives

Good and **bad** have irregular comparative adjective forms.

good → better — Adjectives

bad → worse — Comparative adjectives

Further examples

The tree is **bigger than** the flower.

Our cat is much **lazier than** our dog.

The weather was bad yesterday, but today it's **worse**.

TIP!
You can say **much** before a comparative adjective to make it stronger. Go to 71.2 to find out more.

My bike is much **cleaner** than yours.

I'm quite good at the violin, and I'm getting **better**.

64.4 How to form: Long comparative adjectives

With most two-syllable adjectives and all adjectives with three or more syllables, put **more** in front of the adjective and don't add **er**. Use **less** in front of any adjective to give the opposite meaning to **more**.

comparative adjective

subject + verb	more/less	adjective	than	rest of sentence
The rocket is	more less	expensive	than	the robot.

Further examples

I think board games are **more exciting than** video games.

The red flower is beautiful, but the purple flower is **more beautiful.**

This puzzle is **less difficult than** that puzzle.

TIP!
A syllable is a part of a word. Each vowel sound in a word is a syllable. Go to R4 to find out more.

The pizzas were **more delicious than** the sandwiches.

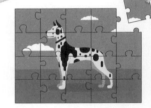

The purple snake is **more colorful than** the green snake.

See also:
Adjectives **63**
Syllables **R4**

65 Superlative adjectives

I am tall. Sofia is taller than me. Max is the tallest.

65.1 How to form: Superlative adjectives

To make superlative adjectives for most one-syllable adjectives and some two-syllable adjectives, add **est** to the adjective.

subject	verb	the	superlative adjective
I	am	the	tallest.

Put **the** before a superlative adjective.

Add **est** to the adjective, **tall**.

When to use
Use **superlative adjectives** to talk about extremes.

65.2 Spelling rules: Superlative adjectives

To form these superlative adjectives, add **est** to the adjective. Sometimes, the spelling of the adjective changes a little before we add **est**.

Adjective ends consonant, vowel, consonant.

tall
→
tallest
For most adjectives, add **est**.

close
→
closest
Just add st.

early
→
earliest
Change the y to an i, then add **est**.

big
→
biggest
Write the last letter twice, then add **est**.

65.3 How to form: Irregular superlative adjectives
Good and **bad** have irregular superlative adjective forms.

good	bad	] Adjectives
↓	↓
better	worse	] Comparative adjectives
↓	↓
best	worst	] Superlative adjectives

Further examples

Today was **the coldest** day of the year.

The closest park is five minutes from my house.

The black and white dog is **the biggest**.

This is **the worst** cake I've ever tasted.

Saturday was **the sunniest** day this week.

Jess is my **best** friend.

65.4 How to form: Long superlative adjectives

With most two-syllable adjectives and all adjectives with three or more syllables, put **the most** in front of the adjective and don't add **est**. Use **the least** in front of any adjective to give the opposite meaning to **the most**.

superlative adjective

subject + verb	the	most/least	adjective
Sara is	the	most / least	excited.

Further examples

I think math is **the most important** subject at school.

This is **the most interesting** museum in our city.

He is **the least afraid** of spiders.

The Eiffel Tower is **the most famous** landmark in Paris.

That's **the most amazing** rainbow I've ever seen!

TIP!
A syllable is a part of a word. Each vowel sound in a word is a syllable. Go to R4 to find out more.

66 Adverbs of manner

See also:
Adjectives **63**
Intensifiers **71**

Hello.

Hello!

⚙ 66.1 How to form: Adverbs of manner

To make most adverbs of manner, add **ly** to an adjective.
Adverbs come after the verb they are describing. If the verb
has an object, the adverb comes after the object.

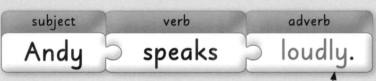

subject	verb	adverb
Andy	speaks	loudly.

Most adverbs of
manner end with **ly**.

When to use
Use **adverbs of manner**
to describe a verb to
say how someone
or something does
something.

⚙ 66.2 Spelling rules: Adverbs of manner

To make most adverbs of manner, add **ly** to an adjective.
Sometimes the spelling of the adjective changes a little
before we add **ly**.

Adjective ends with a y.

Adjective ends
with a consonant
followed by le.

quiet
↓
quietly

For most
adverbs, add **ly**.

easy
↓
easi**ly**

Change the y to
an i, then add **ly**.

gentle
↓
gent**ly**

Drop the e,
then add **y**.

⚙ 66.3 How to form: Irregular adverbs of manner

Some adverbs of manner are irregular. The adverb **well** doesn't look like its adjective, **good**. Some don't change from their adjective form. Here are some common irregular adverbs of manner.

good | straight | fast | hard | early] Adjectives

↓ ↓ ↓ ↓ ↓

well | straight | fast | hard | early] Adverbs

This adverb changes completely.

Some adverbs stay the same as their adjective form.

Adjectives that end with **ly** do not change to become adverbs.

Further examples

The car is moving really **fast**.

Sara stroked the cat **gently**.

She sings **beautifully**.

Ben can play the piano very **well**.

Maria had to get up **early** today.

REMEMBER!
You can say **very** or **really** before an adverb of manner to make it stronger. Go to 71.1 to find out more.

67 Comparative adverbs

See also:
Comparative adjectives **64**
Adverbs of manner **66**

I run quickly, but Sofia runs more quickly.

⚙ 67.1 How to form: Comparative adverbs

To make most comparative adverbs, add **more** or **less** in front of the adverb. Say **more** when someone does something to a greater degree than someone else. **Less** has the opposite meaning.

When to use
Use **comparative adverbs** to compare how two or more people or things do something.

comparative adverb

subject	verb	more/less	adverb
Sofia	runs	more / less	quickly.

Add **more** or **less** before the adverb.

The adverb stays the same.

REMEMBER!
You can say **much** before a comparative adverb to make it stronger. Go to 71.2 to find out more.

When making a comparison with something else, say **than** after the comparative adverb.

subject	verb	more/less	adverb	than	rest of sentence
Sofia	runs	more / less	quickly	than	Max.

Say **than** after the comparative adverb.

67.2 How to form: Irregular comparative adverbs

Good and **bad** have irregular comparative adverb forms.

good → bad] Adjectives

well → badly] Adverbs

better → worse] Comparative adverbs

67.3 How to form: Short comparative adverbs

If an adjective has a comparative form ending with **er**, you can use this instead of **more** plus adverb.

subject + verb	comparative adverb	rest of sentence
Sofia runs	more quickly / quicker	than Max.

More quickly and quicker mean the same thing here.

REMEMBER!
To find out more about comparative adjectives, go to Unit 64.

Further examples

Andy speaks **louder than** Sofia.

Sara paints **more carefully than** me.

Maria plays the violin much **better than** Ben.

This cheese smells **worse than** that cheese.

171

See also:
Superlative adjectives **65**
Adverbs of manner **66**

68 Superlative adverbs

I run the most quickly.

I run the least quickly.

68.1 How to form: Superlative adverbs

To make most superlative adverbs, add **the most**
or **the least** in front of the adverb.

superlative adverb

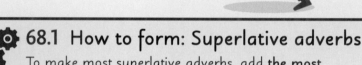

subject	verb	the	most/least	adverb
Sofia	runs	the	most / least	quickly.

Say **the** before
most or least.

The adverb stays
the same.

When to use
Use **superlative adverbs**
to describe extremes in
how things are done.

Use **the most** when someone does something more than anyone else.
Use **the least** when someone does something less than anyone else.

Sofia runs the most quickly.

Andy runs the least quickly.

The least means the
opposite of **the most**.

⚙ 68.2 How to form: Irregular superlative adverbs

Good and **bad** have irregular superlative adverb forms.

good	bad	] Adjectives
↓	↓	
well	badly	] Adverbs
↓	↓	
better	worse	] Comparative adverbs
↓	↓	
best	worst	] Superlative adverbs

⚙ 68.3 How to form: Short superlative adverbs

If an adjective has a superlative form ending in **est**, you can use this instead of **the most** plus adverb.

REMEMBER!
To find out more about superlative adjectives, go to Unit 65.

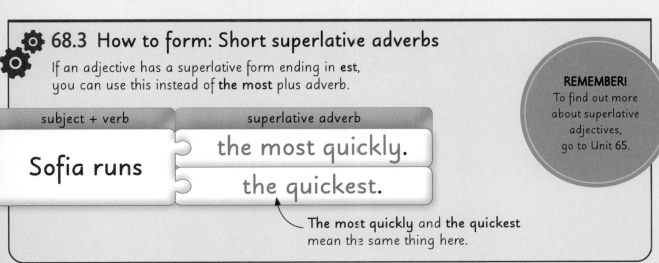

subject + verb	superlative adverb
Sofia runs	the most quickly.
	the quickest.

The most quickly and **the quickest** mean the same thing here.

Further examples

The black dog barks **the most loudly.**

Max swims **the fastest.**

Maria sings **the least beautifully.**

69 Adverbs of time

See also:
Adverbs of frequency **70**
Prepositions of time **74**

Use adverbs of time to talk about an ongoing action in the present or to say exactly when something is happening in the present, happened in the past, or will happen in the future.

69.1 "now"

We're playing video games now.

When to use
Use **now** to talk about something that is happening in the present moment.

PAST   PRESENT   FUTURE

This is happening in the present moment.

69.2 "still"

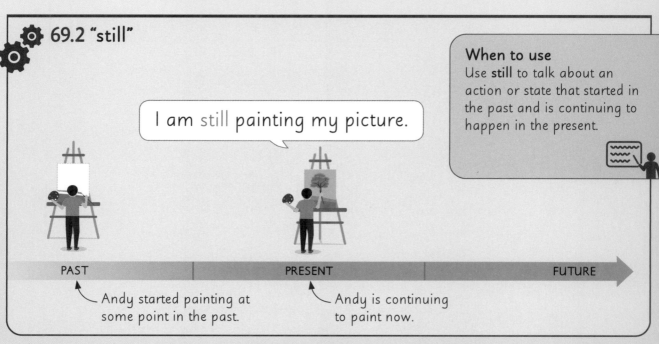

I am still painting my picture.

When to use
Use **still** to talk about an action or state that started in the past and is continuing to happen in the present.

PAST   PRESENT   FUTURE

Andy started painting at some point in the past.

Andy is continuing to paint now.

69.3 "about to"

It's about to rain.

PRESENT — FUTURE

It's going to rain in the very near future.

When to use
Use **about to** to talk about something that is going to happen in the very near future.

69.4 "soon"

I'm going to the beach soon.

PRESENT — FUTURE

Sofia isn't at the beach now.

Sofia will be at the beach in the near future.

When to use
Use **soon** to talk about something that is going to happen in the near future.

69.5 "yet"

I haven't finished my dinner yet.

PRESENT — FUTURE

Andy hasn't finished his dinner.

Andy will finish his dinner at some point.

When to use
Use **yet** in negative sentences and questions to talk about something that hasn't happened, but will happen in the future.

69.6 "just"

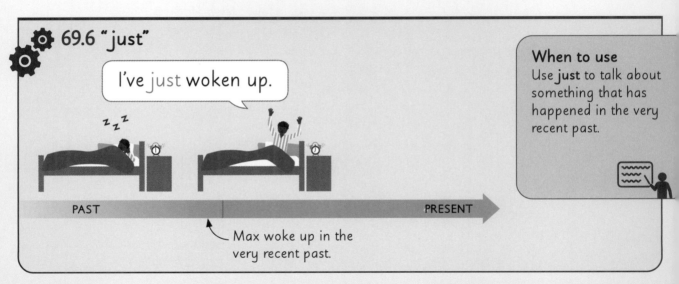

I've **just** woken up.

PAST   PRESENT

Max woke up in the very recent past.

When to use
Use **just** to talk about something that has happened in the very recent past.

69.7 "already"

I've **already** fed the dog.

PAST   PRESENT

Sofia has fed the dog.

When to use
Use **already** to talk about something that has happened in the past, sometimes earlier than you expected.

69.8 "ago"

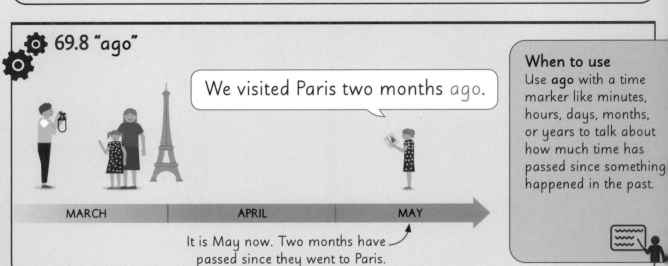

We visited Paris two months **ago**.

MARCH   APRIL   MAY

It is May now. Two months have passed since they went to Paris.

When to use
Use **ago** with a time marker like minutes, hours, days, months, or years to talk about how much time has passed since something happened in the past.

Further examples

now	Use to talk about something that is happening in the present moment.	What are you doing **now**? Sorry, we have got to go **now**.
still	Use to talk about an action or state that started in the past and is ongoing.	They're **still** running the race. It's **still** raining.
about to	Use to talk about something that is going to happen in the very near future.	We're **about to** go shopping. I'm **about to** play ice hockey.
soon	Use to talk about something that is going to happen in the near future.	Dinner will be ready **soon**. Get ready to go, we're leaving **soon**.
yet	Use to talk about something that hasn't happened, but will happen in the future.	Has Andy woken up **yet**? I haven't finished my drawing **yet**.
just	Use to talk about something that has happened in the very recent past.	I've **just** washed the dishes. We've **just** arrived in Miami.
already	Use to talk about something that has happened, sometimes earlier than expected.	I've **already** done my homework. The movie has **already** started.
ago	Use to talk about how much time has passed since something happened.	I took this picture three days **ago**. A week **ago**, we were in Australia.

See also:
Adverbs of time **69**
Prepositions of time **74**

⚙ 70.1 Using adverbs of frequency

Use adverbs of frequency to talk about how often something happens.

100%

I **always brush my teeth in the morning.**

When to use
Use **always** when something happens all the time.

I **usually get up at 7 o'clock.**

Use **usually** when something happens regularly, but not all the time.

I **often have toast for breakfast.**

Use **often** when something happens frequently.

I **sometimes play soccer on Sundays.**

Use **sometimes** when something happens occasionally.

I **never walk to school. It's too far away.**

Use **never** when something doesn't happen at all.

0%

70.2 How to form: Adverbs of frequency

Adverbs of frequency usually go before the main verb.

subject	adverb of frequency	verb	rest of sentence
I	always	read	a book in the evening.

The adverb of frequency goes before the verb.

If the main verb is **to be**, the adverb of frequency goes after **to be**.

subject	to be	adverb of frequency	rest of sentence
I	am	never	late for school.

The adverb of frequency goes after **to be**.

Further examples

We **always** walk the dog in the evening.

Tom **usually** plays baseball on Tuesdays.

They **often** go on vacation to France.

We **sometimes** have pizza for dinner.

He is **never** bored at the park.

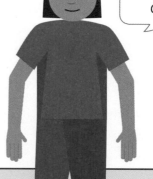

I **never** wear dresses.

See also:
Adjectives **63**
Adverbs of manner **66**

The gray dog is dirty.
The brown dog is very dirty.

71.1 "very" and "really"

Use **very** or **really** before an adjective or an adverb.

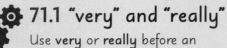

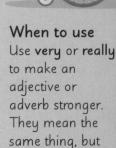

subject	verb	very/really	adjective
The brown dog	is	very / really	dirty.

Put **very** or **really** before an adjective or adverb.

subject	verb	very/really	adverb
The brown dog	walks	very / really	slowly.

When to use
Use **very** or **really** to make an adjective or adverb stronger. They mean the same thing, but **really** is a bit more informal.

Further examples

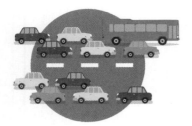

The road is **very** busy.

Maria's dad is **really** tall.

Sofia can run **really** fast.

The gray dog is much bigger than the black dog.

71.2 "much"
Use **much** before a comparative adjective or a comparative adverb.

When to use
Use **much** to make a comparative adjective or adverb stronger.

subject	verb	much	comparative adjective
The gray dog	is	much	bigger.

Put **much** before the comparative adjective.

subject	verb	much	comparative adverb
The gray dog	barks	much	more loudly.

Put **much** before the comparative adverb.

Further examples

The rabbit runs **much** more quickly than the tortoise.

It's **much** colder in winter than in summer.

The drums are **much** noisier than the guitar.

Prepositions of place

See also:
Prepositions of movement **73**
Prepositions of time **74**

 72.1 Using prepositions of place

Use prepositions of place to talk about where someone or something is.

The cat is
in the box.

The cat is
on the box.

The cat is
next to the box.

The cat is
in front of the box.

The cat is
behind the box.

The cat is
opposite the box

The cat is
between the boxes.

The cat is
under the plant.

The cat is
below the tree.

The bird is
above the cat.

73 Prepositions of movement

See also:
Prepositions of place **72**
Prepositions of time **74**

73.1 Using prepositions of movement

Use prepositions of movement to talk about how someone or something moves from one place to another.

The cat is walking **up** the stairs.

The cat is walking **down** the stairs.

The cat is jumping **into** the box.

The cat is jumping **out of** the box.

The cat is jumping **over** the box.

The cat is walking **under** the desk.

The cat is jumping **off** the box.

The cat is walking **through** the box.

The cat is walking **across** the yard.

Prepositions of time

Use prepositions of time to talk about when something happens.

74.1 "on"

We play basketball on Saturdays.

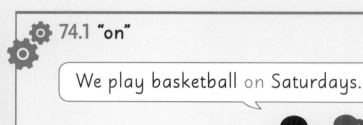

When to use
Use **on** before a day of the week or a date to say when something happens, happened, or will happen.

74.2 "at"

I get up at 7 o'clock.

When to use
Use **at** before a time to say when something happens, happened, or will happen.

74.3 "in"

My birthday is in May.

May

When to use
Use **in** before months; years; seasons; and the words **morning**, **afternoon**, and **evening** to say when something happens, happened, or will happen.

See also:
Adverbs of time **69**
Time words **R28**

74.4 "until"

You can play until dinner.

When to use
Use **until** with a time, date, year, or event to talk about when an ongoing action or situation will finish.

NOW

UNTIL

They are going to stop playing before dinner.

74.5 "from... to..."

We go to gymnastics from 10 o'clock to 1 o'clock.

When to use
Use **from... to...** with times to talk about when something starts and finishes.

FROM

TO

The activity starts at 10 o'clock.

The activity finishes at 1 o'clock.

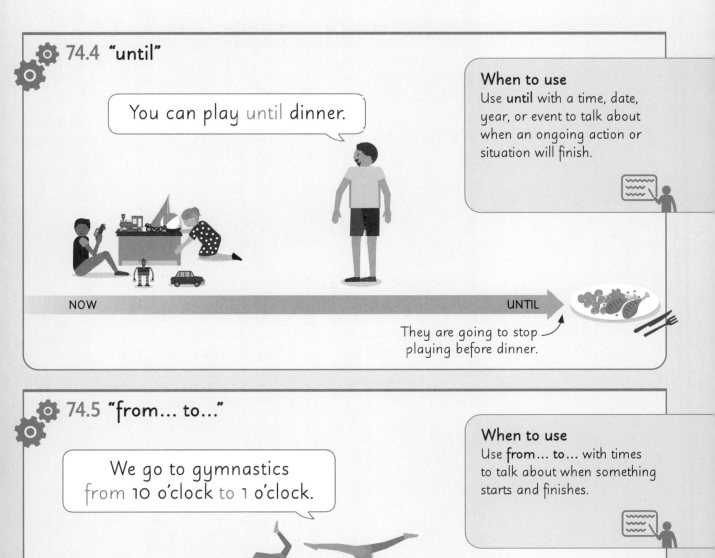

74.6 "for"

When to use
Use **for** before an amount of time to talk about how long something happens.

We played chess for two hours today.

FOR TWO HOURS

They started playing chess at 4 o'clock.

They finished playing chess at 6 o'clock.

74.7 "since"

When to use
Use **since** to talk about when an ongoing action or situation started. Use **since** with the present perfect, never the present simple.

We've been at the fair since 11 o'clock.

SINCE

NOW

The activity started at 11 o'clock and is ongoing.

74.8 "during"

When to use
Use **during** to talk about the period of time when something happens.

> I went to the library **during** my lunch break.

PAST   DURING LUNCH BREAK   NOW

Sara was in the library at some point while it was her lunch break.

74.9 "by"

When to use
Use **by** with a time to say that something will be done or finished before that time.

> I have to be home **by** 6 o'clock.

NOW   BY 6 O'CLOCK

Max has to be home between now and 6 o'clock.

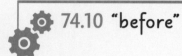

74.10 "before"

We usually walk the
dog before dinner.

When to use
Use **before** to talk about
something that happens sooner
than something else.

BEFORE DINNER   DINNER

This means that they walk the
dog first, then they have dinner.

74.11 "after"

I often read comic
books after dinner.

When to use
Use **after** to talk about
something that happens later
than something else.

DINNER   AFTER DINNER

This means that Max eats dinner
first, then he reads comic books.

Further examples

on	Use with a day or date to say when something happens.	I go to science club **on** Wednesdays. We played badminton **on** Friday.
at	Use with a time to say when something happens.	We eat breakfast **at** 7 o'clock. I catch the bus **at** 8 o'clock.
in	Use with some time words to say when something happens.	I was born **in** the summer. My school has a party every year **in** July.
until	Use with some time words to say when something will finish.	I have basketball practice **until** 4 o'clock. We have to stay here **until** we've finished.
from... to...	Use with times to say when something starts and finishes.	My Dad works **from** 9 o'clock **to** 5 o'clock. Lunchtime is **from** 12 o'clock **to** 1 o'clock.
since	Use to talk about when something ongoing started.	I've been here **since** 3 o'clock. We've been in Spain **since** last week.
for	Use to talk about how long something happens.	I have been at school **for** three hours. We played **for** two hours yesterday.
during	Use to talk about the period of time when something happens.	We played all day **during** the summer. Andy learned a lot **during** the lesson.
by	Use to say what time something will be finished before.	I have to finish my homework **by** 6 o'clock. We've usually eaten dinner **by** 7 o'clock.
before	Use to talk about something that happens sooner.	I eat breakfast **before** school. Sara has soccer practice **before** dinner.
after	Use to talk about something that happens later.	We're going to the park **after** school. **After** breakfast, I catch the bus.

75 "with" and "without"

With and **without** are prepositions.
They come before a noun.

⚙ 75.1 "with"

Max came with
me to the park.

> **When to use**
> Use **with** to talk about
> something that is present
> with something else.

We stayed at a hotel
with a swimming pool.

> Use **with** to talk about
> possession.

Dad cut the apple
with a knife.

> Use **with** to talk about
> something which is used
> to perform an action.

⚙ 75.2 "without"

I had some ice cream
without **sauce.**

> **When to use**
> Use **without** to talk about
> the absence of something.

Further examples

Do you want to come to the movies **with** us?

I'm going to buy a new toy **with** my money.

Mom made pasta **with** meatballs.

I like books **with** lots of pictures.

We drew our pictures **with** pencils.

They live in a house **with** a yard.

My dad likes tea **without** sugar.

Sara went to school **without** her books.

I prefer burgers **without** cheese.

76 Conjunctions

See also:
Clauses R6

Conjunctions join words, phrases, clauses, or sentences together.

76.1 "and"

I like cars. I like rockets.

I like cars and rockets.

Use **and** to join two sentences together.

When to use
Use **and** to talk about more than one thing or to join two sentences together that are talking about the same thing.

76.2 "but"

I like apples. I don't like pears.

I like apples, but I don't like pears.

Use **but** to contrast a positive statement with a negative statement.

When to use
Use **but** to contrast a positive statement with a negative statement.

76.3 "or"

I don't like dolls. I don't like cars.

I don't like dolls **or** cars.

Use **or** to join two negative
sentences together.

When to use
Use **or** to talk about two
negative statements
together in one sentence.

Would you like pasta? Would you like pizza?

Would you like pasta **or** pizza?

This means there is a choice
between pasta and pizza.

Use **or** when there's a
choice between two or
more things.

76.4 "than"

subject + verb	comparative	than	rest of sentence
Your doll is	smaller	than	mine.

This is a comparative adjective.

Say **than** after a
comparative adjective
or adverb.

When to use
Use **than** to compare two or more things. Use it
after a comparative adjective or adverb. Go to
Units 64 and 67 to find out more about
comparative adjectives and adverbs.

⚙ 76.5 "when"

This happened immediately
after the first action.

when	first action	second action
When	we got to the beach,	we went swimming.

This action happened first.

When to use
Use **when** to talk about two things
that happen at the same time or
immediately after one another.

when	ongoing action	interrupting action
When	I was playing tennis,	I hurt my knee.

The ongoing
action is in the
past continuous.

The interrupting action is
in the past simple.

Use **when** to talk about an
action that happened during
another action.

when	first future event	second future event
When	I get home,	I'll do my homework.

This clause is in the present simple even
though it is happening in the future.

You can also use **when** in the middle of each of these sentences.

I'll do my homework when I get home.

There is no comma
when **when** is in the
middle of the sentence.

Use **when** to talk about
what will happen once
something else happens.

194

76.6 "after"

You can use **after** at the start of a sentence or in the middle of a sentence.

after	first action	second action
After	I get up,	I brush my teeth.

This action happens first.

This action happens second.

I brush my teeth after I get up.

There is no comma when **after** is in the middle of the sentence.

When to use
Use **after** to talk about something that happens later than another action.

76.7 "before"

You can use **before** at the start of a sentence or in the middle of a sentence.

before	second action	first action
Before	I go to sleep,	I always read a book.

This action happens second.

This action happens first.

I always read a book before I go to sleep.

There is no comma when **before** is in the middle of the sentence.

When to use
Use **before** to talk about something that happens earlier than another action.

76.8 "if"

You can use **if** at the start of a sentence or in the middle of a sentence.

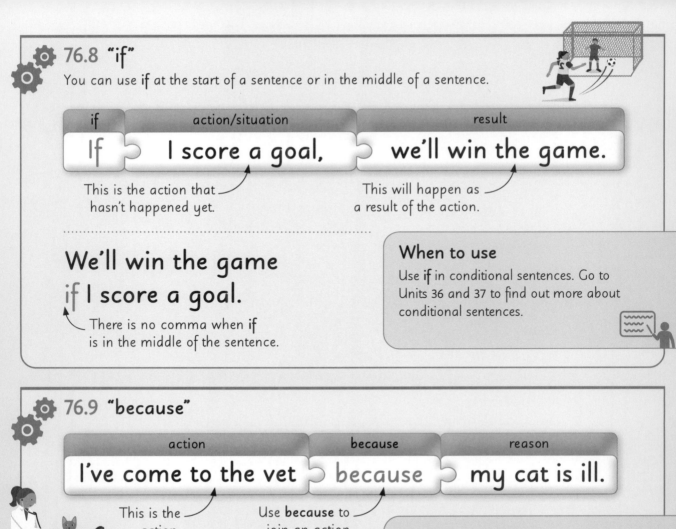

if	action/situation	result
If	I score a goal,	we'll win the game.

This is the action that hasn't happened yet.

This will happen as a result of the action.

We'll win the game if I score a goal.

There is no comma when **if** is in the middle of the sentence.

When to use
Use **if** in conditional sentences. Go to Units 36 and 37 to find out more about conditional sentences.

76.9 "because"

action	because	reason
I've come to the vet	because	my cat is ill.

This is the action.

Use **because** to join an action to its reason.

When to use
Use **because** to say why something happens or to explain a decision.

76.10 "so"

This happened as a result of the situation.

situation/action	so	result
It's sunny today,	so	we've come to the beach.

This is the situation.

When to use
Use **so** to talk about something that happens because of something else.

Further examples

and	Joins two sentences together that are talking about the same thing.	Maria is wearing a red dress **and** blue shoes. I bought Ben a new toy **and** he loved it!
but	Contrasts a positive statement with a negative statement.	I love swimming, **but** I don't like running. She can't sing, **but** she can play the piano.
or	Two or more things in a negative sentence or choice between things.	I've never been to Spain **or** Italy. Do you want to play baseball **or** basketball?
than	Use after a comparative adjective or adverb.	My dog is bigger **than** my cat. Max can run faster **than** Andy.
when	Says at what time something happens.	**When** she got home, she practiced the violin. I'll swim in the ocean **when** I go on vacation.
after	Describes an action that happens later than another action.	Sofia went to bed **after** she ate her dinner. **After** I ran the race, I had a glass of water.
before	Describes an action that happens earlier than another action.	I put on my pajamas **before** I went to bed. **Before** Maria went outside, she put on a coat.
if	Use in conditional sentences.	Don't go to school **if** you're feeling sick. **If** you clean your room, we'll go to the park.
because	Says why something happens or explains a decision.	I love reading **because** it's fun. We didn't walk to school **because** it's raining.
so	Use to talk about something that happens because of something else.	I was hungry, **so** I made a sandwich. Sara was tired, **so** she went to bed early.

Reference

R1 The English alphabet

The English alphabet has 26 letters. It has five vowels, **a**, **e**, **i**, **o**, and **u**.
The other 21 letters are called consonants.

Use a capital letter for the first letter of a sentence,
people's names, place names, days, and months.

Use lowercase letters
the rest of the time.

Aa Bb Cc Dd Ee Ff Gg Hh Ii

Jj Kk Ll Mm Nn Oo Pp Qq Rr

Ss Tt Uu Vv Ww Xx Yy Zz

R2 Punctuation marks

English uses various punctuation marks to make sentences clearer.

Punctuation mark		Use	Example sentence
period	.	comes at the end of a sentence	Maria likes oranges.
comma	,	joins two main clauses or separates words in a list	I like pizza, but I don't like pasta. I love cars, trains, and rockets!
question mark	?	comes at the end of a question	Do you like robots?
exclamation mark	!	comes at the end of a sentence that expresses emotions like excitement	Let's play soccer!
apostrophe	,	shows possession or replaces missing letters in contractions	Ben's cat is black. She's my sister.

R3 Parts of speech

The different types of words that form sentences are called parts of speech.

Part of speech	Definition	Examples
noun	a person, place, or thing	cat, Sara, girl, house, water
adjective	describes a noun or pronoun	big, funny, light, red, young
verb	shows an action or a state of being	be, go, read, speak, think, want
adverb	describes verbs, adjectives, and other adverbs	always, easily, happily, here, loudly, much, soon, very
pronoun	takes the place of a noun	he, she, you, we, them, it
preposition	describes where something is, where something is going, time, or can introduce an object or idea	about, above, from, in
conjunction	a joining word that links words, phrases, or clauses	and, because, but
article	comes before a noun to say whether the noun is specific or general	a, an, some, the
determiner	comes before a noun to show which thing or things you are talking about	her, my, their, your

R4 Syllables

A syllable is a part of a word. Each vowel sound in a word is a syllable. A vowel sound is part of a word that includes a, e, i, o, u, and sometimes y.

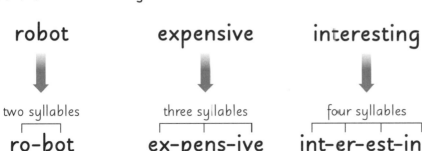

robot   expensive   interesting

↓   ↓   ↓

two syllables   three syllables   four syllables

ro-bot   ex-pens-ive   int-er-est-ing

R5 Parts of a sentence

All sentences have a verb and most have at least a subject, too.
Sentences can contain a direct object.

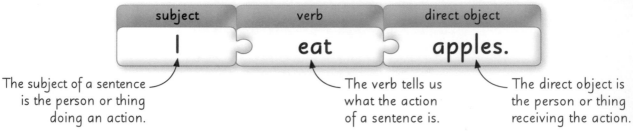

subject	verb	direct object
I	eat	apples.

The subject of a sentence is the person or thing doing an action.

The verb tells us what the action of a sentence is.

The direct object is the person or thing receiving the action.

Sentences can also contain an indirect object. For a sentence to have an indirect object, it must also have a direct object.

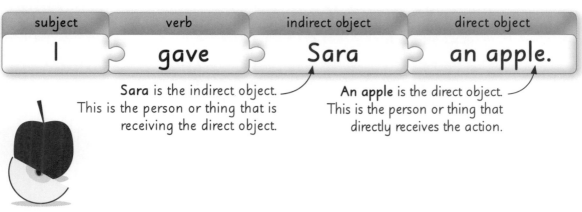

subject	verb	indirect object	direct object
I	gave	Sara	an apple.

Sara is the indirect object. This is the person or thing that is receiving the direct object.

An apple is the direct object. This is the person or thing that directly receives the action.

R6 Clauses

A clause is a phrase that contains a subject and a verb.
Some sentences contain two or more clauses. Clauses can
be joined together by conjunctions and relative pronouns.

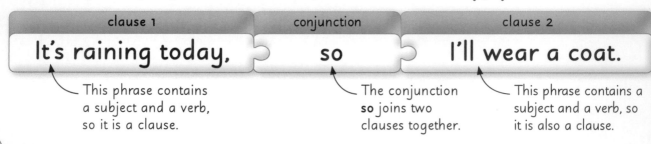

clause 1	conjunction	clause 2
It's raining today,	so	I'll wear a coat.

This phrase contains a subject and a verb, so it is a clause.

The conjunction **so** joins two clauses together.

This phrase contains a subject and a verb, so it is also a clause.

R7 The present simple of regular verbs

Use the present simple to talk about facts, opinions, or things that happen regularly.
Regular verbs all follow the same pattern in the present simple. Go to Unit 1 to find out more.

Positive	Negative	Question
I like	I don't like	Do I like...?
You like	You don't like	Do you like...?
He likes	He doesn't like	Does he like...?
She likes	She doesn't like	Does she like...?
It likes	It doesn't like	Does it like...?
We like	We don't like	Do we like...?
You like	You don't like	Do you like...?
They like	They don't like	Do they like...?

R8 The present simple of "to be"

To be is an irregular verb in the present simple—it doesn't follow the usual rules. Use the present simple of **to be** to talk about facts, feelings, situations, and states. Go to Unit 1 to find out more.

Positive	Negative	Question
I am/I'm	I'm not	Am I...?
You are/You're	You're not/You aren't	Are you...?
He is/He's	He's not/He isn't	Is he...?
She is/She's	She's not/She isn't	Is she...?
It is/It's	It's not/It isn't	Is it...?
We are/We're	We're not/We aren't	Are we...?
You are/You're	You're not/You aren't	Are you...?
They are/They're	They're not/They aren't	Are they...?

R9 The present simple of "to have"

To have is an irregular verb in the present simple—it doesn't follow the usual rules.
Use the present simple of **to have** to talk about possession. Go to Unit 1 to find out more.

Positive	Negative	Question
I have	I don't have	Do I have…?
You have	You don't have	Do you have…?
He has	He doesn't have	Does he have…?
She has	She doesn't have	Does she have…?
It has	It doesn't have	Does it have…?
We have	We don't have	Do we have…?
You have	You don't have	Do you have…?
They have	They don't have	Do they have…?

R10 The present continuous

Use the present continuous to talk about an action that is happening
in the present moment. Go to Unit 4 to find out more.

Positive	Negative	Question
I am walking/I'm walking	I'm not walking	Am I walking?
You are walking/You're walking	You're not walking/You aren't walking	Are you walking?
He is walking/He's walking	He's not walking/He isn't walking	Is he walking?
She is walking/She's walking	She's not walking/She isn't walking	Is she walking?
It is walking/It's walking	It's not walking/It isn't walking	Is it walking?
We are walking/We're walking	We're not walking/We aren't walking	Are we walking?
You are walking/You're walking	You're not walking/You aren't walking	Are you walking?
They are walking/They're walking	They're not walking/They aren't walking	Are they walking?

R11 The past simple of regular verbs

Use the past simple to talk about a finished action that happened at a fixed moment in the past. Go to Unit 8 to find out more. For a list of irregular verbs in the past simple, go to R19.

Positive	Negative	Question
I played	I didn't play	Did I play…?
You played	You didn't play	Did you play…?
He played	He didn't play	Did he play…?
She played	She didn't play	Did she play…?
It played	It didn't play	Did it play…?
We played	We didn't play	Did we play…?
You played	You didn't play	Did you play…?
They played	They didn't play	Did they play…?

R12 The past simple of "to be"

To be is an irregular verb in the past simple—it doesn't follow the usual rules. Use the past simple of to be to talk about facts, feelings, situations, and states. Go to Unit 8 to find out more.

Positive	Negative	Question
I was	I wasn't	Was I…?
You were	You weren't	Were you…?
He was	He wasn't	Was he…?
She was	She wasn't	Was she…?
It was	It wasn't	Was it…?
We were	We weren't	Were we…?
You were	You weren't	Were you…?
They were	They weren't	Were they…?

R13 The past continuous

Use the past continuous to talk about an ongoing action
in the past or to tell a story. Go to Unit 11 to find out more.

Positive	Negative	Questions
I was running	I wasn't running	Was I running?
You were running	You weren't running	Were you running?
He was running	He wasn't running	Was he running?
She was running	She wasn't running	Was she running?
It was running	It wasn't running	Was it running?
We were running	We weren't running	Were we running?
You were running	You weren't running	Were you running?
They were running	They weren't running	Were they running?

R14 The present perfect

Use the present perfect to talk about the recent past. Go to Unit 14 to find out more.
For a list of irregular past participles, go to R19.

Positive	Negative	Questions
I have arrived	I haven't arrived	Have I arrived?
You have arrived	You haven't arrived	Have you arrived?
He has arrived	He hasn't arrived	Has he arrived?
She has arrived	She hasn't arrived	Has she arrived?
It has arrived	It hasn't arrived	Has it arrived?
We have arrived	We haven't arrived	Have we arrived?
You have arrived	You haven't arrived	Have you arrived?
They have arrived	They haven't arrived	Have they arrived?

R15 "Going to"

Use **going to** with a base form to make predictions based on evidence
and to talk about future plans. Go to Unit 18 to find out more.

Positive	Negative	Question
I'm going to swim	I'm not going to swim	Am I going to swim?
You're going to…	You're not going to…/You aren't going to…	Are you going to…?
He's going to…	He's not going to…/He isn't going to…	Is he going to…?
She's going to…	She's not going to…/She isn't going to…	Is she going to…?
It's going to…	It's not going to…/It isn't going to…	Is it going to…?
We're going to…	We're not going to…/We aren't going to…	Are we going to…?
You're going to…	You're not going to…/You aren't going to…	Are you going to…?
They're going to…	They're not going to…/They aren't going to…	Are they going to…?

R16 "Will"

Use **will** with a base form to talk about a decision you've just made, to make a promise, to make
predictions without evidence, or to offer to do something.. Go to Unit 21 to find out more.

Positive	Negative	Question
I will play/I'll play	I will not play/I won't play	Will I play?
You will…/You'll…	You will not…/You won't…	Will you…?
He will…/He'll…	He will not…/He won't…	Will he…?
She will…/She'll…	She will not…/She won't…	Will she…?
It will…/It'll…	It will not…/It won't…	Will it…?
We will…/We'll…	We will not…/We won't…	Will we…?
You will…/You'll…	You will not…/You won't…	Will you…?
They will…/They'll…	They will not…/They won't…	Will they…?

R17 Modal verbs

Modal verbs stay the same for all subjects. Do not add an **s** for **he, she,** or **it**. They are usually followed by another verb in its base form. Questions with **might** and **must** are rare. There is no contraction for **may not**, and **mightn't** and **mustn't** are rare. Go to Unit 28 to find out more.

Positive	Negative	Questions
can	cannot/can't	Can I...?
could	could not/couldn't	Could I...?
may	may not	May I...?
might	might not	
must	must not	
should	should not/shouldn't	Should I...?

R18 Question words

Use question words at the start of a questions. Go to Unit 40 to find out more.

Question word	Example question	Example answer
How	**How** old are you?	I am nine years old.
How many	**How many** ducks are there?	There are five.
How much	**How much** flour do we have?	We have 1 pound.
What	**What** is that?	It's a crocodile.
When	**When** do you play badminton?	I play badminton on Saturdays.
Where	**Where** is the cat?	It is under the table.
Which	**Which** dog is yours?	Rex is my dog.
Who	**Who** is that?	It is Ben.
Whose	**Whose** camera is this?	It is mine.
Why	**Why** do you like soccer?	It is fun!

R19 Irregular verbs

Some verbs in English have irregular past simple forms and past participles.
These are some of the most common ones.

Base form	Past simple	Past participle
be	was/were	been
break	broke	broken
catch	caught	caught
choose	chose	chosen
come	came	come
do	did	done
draw	drew	drawn
drink	drank	drunk
eat	ate	eaten
find	found	found
forget	forgot	forgotten
get	got	gotten
give	gave	given
go	went	gone
have	had	had
hold	held	held
know	knew	known
learn	learned	learned
lose	lost	lost
make	made	made
put	put	put
read	read	read
run	ran	run
say	said	said
see	saw	seen
sleep	slept	slept
swim	swam	swum
tell	told	told
wear	wore	worn
write	wrote	written

R20 Contractions

We often shorten some verbs, especially when we're talking.
These are some of the most common contractions in English.

Pronoun	to be	to have
I	I am ➡ I'm	I have ➡ I've
he	he is ➡ he's	he has ➡ he's
she	she is ➡ she's	she has ➡ she's
it	it is ➡ it's	it has ➡ it's
we	we are ➡ we're	we have ➡ we've
you	you are ➡ you're	you have ➡ you've
they	they are ➡ they're	they have ➡ they've
that	that is ➡ that's	that has ➡ that's
who	who is ➡ who's	who has ➡ who's

Pronoun	will	would
I	I will ➡ I'll	I would ➡ I'd
he	he will ➡ he'll	he would ➡ he'd
she	she will ➡ she'll	she would ➡ she'd
it	it will ➡ it'll	it would ➡ it'd
we	we will ➡ we'll	we would ➡ we'd
you	you will ➡ you'll	you would ➡ you'd
they	they will ➡ they'll	they would ➡ they'd
that	that will ➡ that'll	that would ➡ that'd
who	who will ➡ who'll	who would ➡ who'd

R21 Contractions: verb + "not"

We often shorten verbs followed by **not**, especially when we're talking.

Verb + not					
is not	➡ isn't	had not	➡ hadn't	cannot	➡ can't
are not	➡ aren't	will not	➡ won't	must not	➡ mustn't
was not	➡ wasn't	would not	➡ wouldn't	might not	➡ mightn't
were not	➡ weren't	do not	➡ don't	could not	➡ couldn't
have not	➡ haven't	does not	➡ doesn't	should not	➡ shouldn't
has not	➡ hasn't	did not	➡ didn't		

R22 Pronouns, possessive adjectives, and possessive pronouns

To find out more about subject pronouns, go to Unit 51. To find out more about object pronouns, go to Unit 52. To find out more about possessive adjectives, go to Unit 55. To find out more about possessive pronouns, go to Unit 56. There is no possessive pronoun for **it**.

Subject pronoun	Object pronoun	Possessive adjective	Possessive pronoun
I	me	my	mine
you	you	your	yours
he	him	his	his
she	her	her	hers
it	it	its	
we	us	our	ours
you	you	your	yours
they	them	their	theirs

R23 Spelling rules: Present participles and gerunds

The present participle and gerund form of a verb are always the same. To make them, add **ing** to the base form of the verb. Sometimes the spelling of the base form changes before we add **ing**.

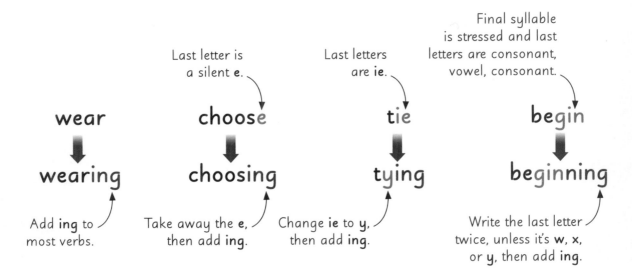

Last letter is a silent **e**.

Last letters are **ie**.

Final syllable is stressed and last letters are consonant, vowel, consonant.

wear → wearing

choose → choosing

tie → tying

begin → beginning

Add **ing** to most verbs.

Take away the **e**, then add **ing**.

Change **ie** to **y**, then add **ing**.

Write the last letter twice, unless it's **w**, **x**, or **y**, then add **ing**.

R24 Spelling rules: Regular past simple and past participles

For regular verbs, their past simple and past participle forms are always the same. To make them, add **ed** to the base form of the verb. Sometimes the spelling of the base form changes before we add **ed**.

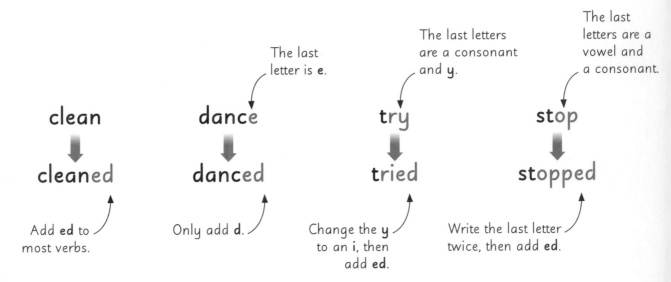

The last letter is **e**.

The last letters are a consonant and **y**.

The last letters are a vowel and a consonant.

clean → cleaned

dance → danced

try → tried

stop → stopped

Add **ed** to most verbs.

Only add **d**.

Change the **y** to an **i**, then add **ed**.

Write the last letter twice, then add **ed**.

R25 Spelling rules: Plural nouns

Most plural nouns are formed by adding an **s** or **es** to the end of a singular noun.

Add **es** to nouns that end with **s**, **x**, **z**, **ch**, or **sh**.

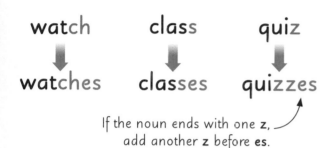

watch → watches

class → classes

quiz → quizzes

If the noun ends with one **z**, add another **z** before **es**.

Add **es** to most nouns that end with **o**. If there's another vowel before the **o**, just add **s**.

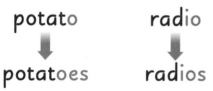

potato → potatoes

radio → radios

For nouns that end with a consonant, then **y**, change the **y** to an **i** then add **es**.

dictionary → dictionaries

story → stories

R26 Irregular plural nouns

Some plural nouns are irregular. They are spelled differently or don't change at all.

Singular		Plural	
mouse		mice	
tooth		teeth	
foot		feet	
child		children	
woman		women	
man		men	
person		people	
sheep		sheep	
fish		fish	

R27 Conjunctions

Use conjunctions to join words, phrases, or clauses together.

Conjunction	Use	Example
after	Use **after** to talk about something that happens later than another action.	I get dressed **after** I eat breakfast.
and	Use **and** to talk about more than one thing or to join two sentences or clauses together	I play the guitar **and** the piano.
because	Use **because** to say why something happens or to explain a decision.	I'm wearing a sweater **because** it's cold.
before	Use **before** to talk about something that happens earlier than another action.	**Before** I have dinner, I wash my hands.
but	Use **but** to contrast a positive statement and a negative statement or to give extra information.	I like robots, **but** I don't like trains.
if	Use **if** in conditional sentences when you're talking about the result of an action, or what might happen when something else happens.	We'll go to the lake **if** it's sunny tomorrow.
or	Use **or** to talk about two or more things in a negative sentence or when there's a choice between two or more things.	I don't like pasta **or** rice. Would you like milk **or** juice?
so	Use **so** to talk about something that happens because of something else.	I'm really tired, **so** I'll go to bed early.
than	Use **than** to compare two or more things. It is used with comparative adjectives and comparative adverbs.	My cat is older **than** my dog.
when	Use **when** to talk about two things that happen at the same time, or if something happens during another action.	**When** we got to the park, we flew our kites.

R28 Time words

Use time words to talk about when things happen. They can be prepositions, conjunctions, or adverbs.

Time word	Use	Example
about to	Use when something is going to happen in the very near future.	I'm **about to** eat dinner.
after	Use when something happens later than something else.	**After** school, I'm going to watch TV.
ago	Use with a time marker to say how much time has passed since something happened.	We got a dog a month **ago**.
already	Use when something has happened.	School has **already** started.
always	Use when something happens all the time.	I **always** wake up early.
at	Use before a time to say when something happens.	School starts **at** 9 o'clock.
before	Use when something happens earlier than something else.	We put our coats on **before** going outside.
by	Use to say when something will be finished.	I need to finish this **by** 6 o'clock.
during	Use to say when something happens.	You shouldn't talk **during** class.
for	Use to say how long something happens.	I read **for** two hours today.
from... to...	Use with times to say when something starts and finishes.	I played video games **from** 7 o'clock **to** 8 o'clock.
in	Use before months, years, and seasons to say when something happens.	It's usually very cold **in** winter.
just	Use when something happened very recently.	I have **just** arrived home.
now	Use when something is happening currently.	We're playing in the park **now**.
on	Use before a day of the week or a date to say when something happens.	We went to the lake **on** Saturday.
since	Use to say when an ongoing action started.	We've been playing **since** 4 o'clock.
soon	Use when something is going to happen in the near future.	I'm going to go swimming **soon**.
still	Use when an ongoing action started in the past.	We're **still** washing the car.
until	Use to say when an ongoing action will finish.	I'm going to draw **until** 5 o'clock.
yet	Use when something hasn't happened.	I haven't gotten dressed **yet**.

Glossary

adjective
A word that describes a *noun* or *pronoun*, e.g. quick.

adverb
A word that describes a *verb*, *adjective*, or another adverb, e.g. quickly, very

adverb of frequency
An adverb that tells you "how often," e.g. usually.

adverb of manner
An adverb that tells you "how," e.g. badly.

adverb of time
An adverb that tells you "when," e.g. soon.

apostrophe
The punctuation mark that shows either possession, e.g. John's cat, or a contraction, e.g. I'm happy.

article
The words a, an, some, and the, which show whether something is general or specific.
see also *definite article*, *indefinite article*

auxiliary verb
A verb which is used with another verb, e.g. to form *tenses*, most commonly to be, to do, and to have.
see also *main verb*

base form
The most basic form of a *verb*, e.g. be, run, write.
see also *infinitive*

cardinal number
The numbers used for counting, e.g. one, two.
see also *ordinal number*

clause
A group of words that contains a *verb*.

closed question
A question that can be answered with "yes" or "no," e.g. Are you American?
see also *open question*

comparative adjective
An adjective that compares one thing or group of things with another, e.g. taller.
see also *superlative adjective*

compound tense
A *tense* which uses an *auxiliary verb*, e.g. the *present perfect*: has done.

conditional
The verb structure used when one event or situation depends on another event or situation happening first.
see also *first conditional*, *zero conditional*

conjunction
A word that links two words or groups of words, e.g. and, because, if.

consonant
Most letters/sounds in English, but not a, e, i, o, u.

continuous
Continuous *tenses* express actions that are in progress at a specific time, e.g. I'm writing.
see also *past continuous*, *present continuous*

contraction
Two words that are joined with an *apostrophe* to form one word, e.g. we are > we're.

countable
A *noun* that can be counted, e.g. one book, two books.
see also *uncountable*

definite article
The word the, which specifies the noun that follows it, e.g. the house in the woods.
see also *indefinite article*

demonstrative determiner/ pronoun
Words that specify a *noun* as closer to (this, these) or more distant from (that, those) the speaker, e.g. This watch is cheaper than that one

determiner
A word that comes before a *noun* and identifies it, e.g. the book, this book.

direct object
The person or thing affected by the action of the *verb*, e.g. "him" in We followed him.
see also *indirect object*

first conditional
A sentence with "if" that describes a possible future situation that depends on another situation, e.g. If it rains, I'll stay here.

first person
When a pronoun or possessive adjective refers to the speaker, e.g. "I" in I am happy.
see also *second person*, *third person*

formal
Formal language is used in situations where you don't know the people very well.
see also *informal*

gerund
The -ing form of a *verb*, when it is used as a noun,
e.g. No running.

imperative
An order to someone, e.g. Stop! The imperative is a *verb* on its own in its *base form*.

indefinite article
The words a, an, and some which come before *nouns* to talk about something in general or for the first time, e.g. Can I borrow a pen?
see also *definite article*

indefinite pronoun
A pronoun that does not refer to a specific person or thing, e.g. someone, nothing.

indirect object
The person or thing affected by the action of a *transitive verb*, but is not the direct object, e.g. "the dog" in I gave the ball to the dog.
see also *direct object*

infinitive (to-infinitive)
The *base form* of a *verb*, with the infinitive marker "to," e.g. to go, to run.

informal
Informal language is used in situations where you know the people well and feel relaxed.
see also *formal*

intensifier
A word that makes an adjective or adverb stronger, e.g. very, really, and much.

intransitive verb
A verb that does not take a *direct object*.
see also *transitive verb*

irregular
A word that behaves differently from most words like it, e.g. men is an irregular *plural noun*.
see also *regular*

main clause
A *clause* that could form a complete *sentence* on its own.
see also *subordinate clause*

main verb
The verb in a group of verbs that carries the meaning, e.g. "ride" in I can ride a bike.

modal verb
A type of *auxiliary verb* that is used with a *main verb* to show ideas like ability and permission.

negative
A *sentence* that contains a word like not or never.

noun
A word that refers to a person, place, or thing.

noun phrase
A *noun*, *pronoun*, or a number of words that are linked to a noun, e.g. the blue house.

object
A *noun* or *pronoun* that follows a *verb* or a *preposition*.

object pronoun
A pronoun that usually follows a *verb* or a *preposition*, e.g. me, them.

open question
A question that cannot be answered with "yes" or "no." They start with a *question word*.
see also *closed question*

ordinal number
The numbers used for ordering, e.g. first, second.
see also *cardinal number*

participle
The form of a *verb* used to make *compound tenses*.
see also *past participle* and *present participle*

past continuous
A *tense* that is formed with was or were and the *present participle*, e.g. was doing. It expresses an ongoing action in the past.

past participle
The *participle* form of a *verb* that is used to make *perfect tenses*, e.g. walked, done, eaten.

past simple
A *tense* that consists only of the past form of a *verb*, e.g. walked, said, ate. It expresses a completed action in the past.

perfect
Perfect *tenses* express a link between two times, e.g. the *present perfect* links the past with the present.

person
The form of a *pronoun* that shows who is speaking (I, we), who is being spoken to (you), or who or what is being mentioned (he, she, it, they). *Verbs* also reflect person, e.g. am is the first person singular form of to be.

personal pronoun
A word that refers to people or things that have already been mentioned, e.g. he, they.
see also *object pronouns*, *subject pronouns*

plural
The form of a word used when there is more than one of something, e.g. books, they.
see also *singular*

positive
A *sentence* that expresses what someone or something is or does. It does not contain a negative word.
see also *negative*

possessive adjective
A word that comes before a *noun* and shows possession, e.g. my, our, his.

possessive pronoun
A word that replaces a *noun* and shows possession, e.g. mine, ours, his.

predicate
The part of a *sentence* containing a *verb* that describes what the *subject* of the *sentence* is doing, e.g. "likes apples" in Sara likes apples.

preposition
A short word that links two *nouns* or *pronouns* to show a relationship, e.g. to, at, with, from.

present continuous
A *tense* that is formed with the present of be and the *present participle*, e.g. is doing. It expresses an ongoing action in the present.

present participle
The *participle* form of a *verb* that is used to make *continuous tenses*, e.g. walking, doing.

present perfect
A *tense* that is formed with the present of to have and the *past participle*, e.g. have done. It expresses an action that started in the past and is still continuing or that happened in the past but has a result in the present.

present simple
A *tense* that consists only of the present form of a *verb*, e.g. walk, say, eat. It expresses a general truth, an opinion, or a habit.

pronoun
A word that replaces a *noun*, when the noun has already been mentioned, e.g. it, that.

proper noun
A noun that is the name of a person, places, days, and months, e.g. Maria, France, Sunday. Proper nouns always start with a capital letter.

question
A *sentence* that asks for something, usually information.

question word
A word that is used to start some questions, e.g. what, which, who, why, how.

reflexive pronoun
A word that refers to the *subject* of the *sentence*, when the subject and *object* are the same, e.g. myself.

regular
A word that behaves in the same way as most words like it, e.g. books is a regular *plural noun* and waited is a regular *past simple* form.
see also *irregular*

relative clause
A clause that gives information about the *subject* or *object* of the *main clause*.

relative pronoun
A word that introduces a *relative clause*, e.g. who, that, which, where.

second person
When a pronoun or possessive adjective refers to someone the speaker is directly addressing, e.g. "You" in You are smiling.
see also *first person*, *third person*

sentence
A group of one or more *clauses*.

short answer
An answer to a *question* that only uses the *subject* and *auxiliary verb*, e.g. Yes, I do.

simple tense
Simple *tenses* are formed with a *main verb* only; they don't need an *auxiliary verb* in their *positive* forms.

singular
The form of a word that is used to refer to just one person or thing, e.g. book.
see also *plural*

statement
A *sentence* that offers information, i.e. not a *question* or an *imperative*.

stress
Saying one *syllable* in a word, or one word in a *sentence*, more strongly than the others.

subject
The person, thing, place, etc. that usually comes before the *verb* in a *sentence*.

subject pronoun
A word that replaces a *noun* as the subject of a *sentence*, e.g. I, she, they.

subordinate clause
A *clause* which is dependent on the *main clause*, usually introduced by a *conjunction*.

superlative adjective
An adjective that indicates the most extreme of a group of things, e.g. best.
see also *comparative adjective*

syllable
Every word is made up of a number of syllables, each of which contain a *vowel* sound, e.g. teach (one syllable), teacher (two syllables).

tag question
A short phrase that makes a *statement* into a *question*, e.g. "isn't it" in It's hot today, isn't it?

tense
The form of a *verb* that shows the time of the action, e.g. *present simple*, *past simple*.

third person
When a pronoun, name, or possessive adjective refers to someone who is not the speaker or is not being directly addressed by the speaker, e.g. "They" in They are playing soccer.
see also *first person*, *second person*

time marker
A word or phrase that indicates a time, e.g. now, yesterday, tomorrow.

transitive verb
A verb that takes a *direct object*.
see also *intransitive verb*

uncountable
A *noun* that cannot be counted, e.g. water, money.
see also *countable*

verb
A word that refers to a situation or an action, e.g. stay, write.

vowel
The English letters a, e, i, o, u.
see also *consonant*

word class
Shows the function of a word in a sentence, e.g. *noun*, *verb*, *adjective* are all word classes.

word order
The position that different words have in a *sentence*, e.g. the *subject* usually comes before the *verb*.

zero conditional
A *sentence* with "if" or "when" that describes a present situation or a regular action, e.g. When it rains, we stay inside.

Index

All numbers refer to unit numbers. Unit numbers in black show the main information. Unit numbers starting with an **R** are located in the reference section.

Acknowledgments

The publisher would like to thank:

Oliver Drake, Kayla Dugger, and Lori Hand for proofreading,
Laura Gardner and Jessica Tapolcai for design assistance,
and Elizabeth Wise for indexing.

All images are copyright DK. For more
information, please visit

www.dkimages.com.

WHAT WILL YOU LEARN NEXT?

BOOKS

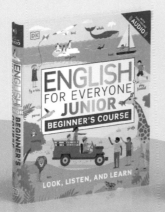

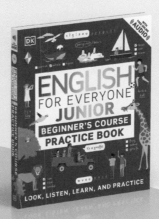

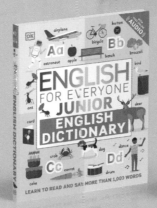

FLASHCARDS